KU-101-922

# 1000 things you should know about

# oceans

# Consultant: Clint Twist

MiLes
KeLLy
PUBLISHING

| WORCESTERSHIRE COUNTY COUNCIL | |
| --- | --- |
| 937 | |
| Bertrams | 18.12.07 |
| J577.7 | £5.99 |
| | |

This material was first published as hardback in 2005

This edition published in 2007 by Miles Kelly Publishing Ltd
Bardfield Centre, Great Bardfield, Essex, CM7 4SL

Copyright © Miles Kelly Publishing Ltd 2005

2 4 6 8 10 9 7 5 3 1

Editorial Director: Belinda Gallagher
Art Director: Jo Brewer
Editor: Rosalind McGuire
Editorial Assistant: Bethanie Bourne
Volume Designer: Ian Paulyn
Reprographics: Anthony Cambray, Stephan Davis,
Liberty Newton, Ian Paulyn

All rights reserved. No part of this publication may be reproduced,
stored in a retrieval system, or transmitted by any means, electronic,
mechanical, photocopying, recording or otherwise, without the prior
permission of the copyright holder.

British Library Cataloguing-in-Publication Data
A catalogue record for this book is available from the British Library

ISBN 978-1-84236-852-7

Printed in China

info@mileskelly.net
www.mileskelly.net

All artworks from the MKP Archives

ACKNOWLEDGEMENTS
The publishers thank the following source for the use of their photograph:
Page 61 (B) Stephen Frink/CORBIS

All other photographs from:
Castrol, CMCD, Corbis, Corel, digitalSTOCK, digitalvision, Flat Earth,
Hemera, ILN, John Foxx, PhotoAlto, PhotoDisc, PhotoEssentials,
PhotoPro, Stockbyte

# CONTENTS

# The blue planet

- **The Earth** is the only planet in the Solar System with enough oxygen and water to support life.

- **At first**, huge numbers of large rocks called meteorites crashed into the Earth. These collisions made round hollows on the surface.

- **Radioactive elements** on the Earth released heat, causing heavy elements such as iron to sink deep into the Earth to form its core.

- **The largest part** of the Earth is a layer called the mantle, which is partially molten. It lies between the core and the crust.

- **Acids in rainwater** corroded the Earth's rocky surface. Chemicals in these rocks were carried into the oceans. Among these were salts that made the ocean water salty.

- **The Earth's surface** cooled and solidified to form the outer layer – the crust. The crust was broken into several fragments ( tectonic plates) that floated on the mantle.

- **These plates** often collided, which built up pressure beneath the crust, leading to cracks on the Earth's surface.

- **Gases and water vapour** burst through the cracks, which slowly led to the formation of the atmosphere.

- **Water vapour** condensed to form clouds that brought rain, but the Earth's surface was so hot that the rainwater evaporated.

- **As the rains** continued the Earth started to cool.

- **The rain** also formed smaller bodies of water such as rivers, lakes and streams.

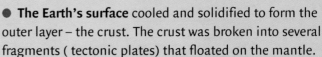

◀ Volcanoes erupted continuously, covering the surface of the Earth with oceans of lava.

# Oceans of the world

- **Water covers** over 360 million sq km of the Earth's surface. It has been divided into five major ocean basins.

- **The five basins** are the Pacific, Atlantic, Indian, Arctic and Antarctic oceans. The Arctic Ocean surrounds the North Pole and is largely frozen.

- **The Pacific Ocean** is the largest. At 166 million sq km, it is twice the size of the Atlantic Ocean.

- **The average depth** of the Pacific Ocean is more than 4000 m, making it the world's deepest ocean.

- **The name** 'Pacific Ocean' comes from the Spanish word 'pacifico', meaning peaceful. It was named by the Portuguese explorer Ferdinand Magellan.

- **The Atlantic Ocean**, at 82 million sq km, is the second largest ocean. It is also the stormiest.

▲ The Pacific Ocean is deep enough to engulf the whole of Mount Everest.

- **The Indian Ocean** has a total area of over 73 million sq km. It is bounded by Asia, Africa and Oceania.

- **Some of the earliest known civilizations**, such as the Mesopotamian, Egyptian and Indus Valley civilizations, developed near the Indian Ocean.

- **The Arctic Ocean**, at 14 million sq km, is both the smallest and shallowest ocean. The deepest point in the Arctic Ocean is only 5450 m.

- **The Antarctic Ocean** is formed by the southern extensions of the Pacific, Atlantic and Indian oceans.

**★ STAR FACT ★**
Some of the most important seas are contained within the Atlantic Ocean, including the Baltic Sea, Black Sea and the Mediterranean Sea.

# Studying the oceans

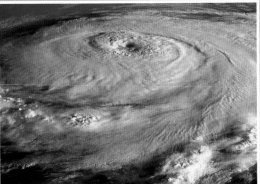

► A satellite photograph of a hurricane forming over the Earth. Meteorological oceanography deals with the influence of oceans on weather patterns across the world.

● **The study** of oceans and their ecosystems is called oceanography.

● **Oceanography** comprises marine geology, physical oceanography, chemical oceanography, marine biology and meteorological oceanography.

● **Marine geology** is the study of tectonic plates. Marine geologists involved in offshore oil exploration and drilling also study how sediments and minerals are formed.

● **Physical oceanography** is the study of the physical processes that take place in the oceans. These include currents, temperature and the causes of tides.

● **Chemical oceanography** is the study of chemicals in the oceans.

● **Oceanography also includes** the study of caves (speleology). This subject deals with the origin, structure and development of caves. It also studies the flora and fauna of caves.

● **Hydrography** is the study of water depth and quality, and the ocean floor, and their impact on navigation.

● **Oceanography gained importance** with the age of discovery in AD 1400–1500.

● **It was during this time** that the oceans were mapped out during this time by explorers.

● **Meteorological oceanography** deals with the interaction between the oceans and the atmosphere. It is the study of atmospheric reactions above the oceans and the influence of the oceans on global weather.

# Ocean floor

● **Oceans cover** about 70 percent of our planet's surface.

● **The surface of the land** under the oceans is called the ocean floor.

● **The ocean floor** is broadly divided into the continental shelf, the continental slope and deep ocean floor.

● **The continental shelf** is an underwater extension of the coast.

● **The outer rims of islands** and continents gently slopes into the surrounding water to form the continental shelf.

● **The average width of the continental shelf** is about 65 km but some, such as the Siberian Shelf in the Arctic Ocean, can extend up to 1500 km.

● **The continental shelf** is commercially very important. It contains large deposits of petroleum, natural gas and minerals. This area also receives the most sunlight and marine life thrives here.

◄ Beneath the oceans is a landscape similar to that found on land.

● **The continental slope** is the point where the shelf starts to plunge towards the ocean floor. The ocean floor is marked by deep canyons.

● **Below continental slopes** sediments often collect to form gentle slopes called continental rise. The continental shelf, slope and rise are together known as continental margin.

● **In many places** the ocean floor forms vast expanses that are flat and covered with sediment. These regions are called the abyssal plains.

● **The abyssal plain** is broken by mid-ocean ridges, such as the Mid-Atlantic and the East Pacific rise, and trenches such as the Mariana Trench in the Pacific Ocean.

# Trenches and ridges

● **The ocean floor** has high mountains, deep valleys, canyons and vast plains.

● **Ocean floor structures** include trenches (similar to valleys) and ridges (similar to mountain chains).

● **The Earth's crust** is made up of huge rock segments (tectonic plates) which move against each other.

● **Ridges and trenches are formed** by the movement of these plates.

● **Ridges form** when two plates drift apart and hot lava oozes through the cracks and cools. A trench forms when a heavy plate plunges beneath a lighter one.

● **Mariana Trench** is one of the deepest trenches. It is located in the Pacific Ocean.

● **The Challenger Deep**, in the Mariana Trench, is the deepest point in the Earth – it is 11,033 m deep.

● **The mid-ocean ridge** is the longest mountain chain on Earth at over 50,000 km long. The crests of these mountains lie nearly 2500 m below the ocean surface.

● **Sometimes the mid-ocean ridge** rises above the sea level. Iceland is located on a crest of the mid-Atlantic ocean ridge.

● **Seamounts are underwater volcanoes.** A flat-topped seamount is known as a guyot, while those with peaks are known as seapeaks.

◀ In 1960, US Navy Leiutenant Don Walsh and Swiss scientist, Jacques Piccard, descended to the bottom of the Challenger Deep, in the US Navy submersible, Trieste.

# Causing waves

● **Oceans are continually** rocked by movements such as waves, currents and tides.

● **Most movements in the oceans** are caused by wind. Waves are created by winds blowing over the surface of the oceans.

● **The water in a wave** moves in circles. As a wave nears land it slows. The top part of the wave continues and crashes on the shore as a breaker.

● **The shape and size of waves differ**. A steep, choppy wave is one that has formed near the coast, while slow, steady waves are those that formed out in the ocean.

● **The regular rise and fall** of the oceans are called tides. They are caused by the gravitational pull of the Sun and the Moon.

● **The period of high water level** is known as high tide and the period of low water level is known as low tide.

● **An ocean current** is a mass of water moving continuously in one direction.

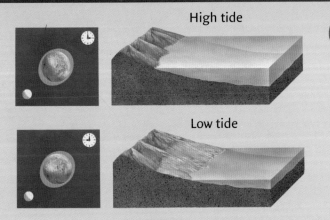

High tide

Low tide

▲ High tide occurs in those areas that are closest to and farthest away from the Moon. As the Earth turns, low tide occurs.

● **Surface currents** are caused by winds and rotation of the Earth.

● **Underwater currents** are caused by differences in temperature and salt content.

● **When the Sun, Moon and Earth** are aligned, their combined gravities cause very high tides (spring tides). Smaller tides (neap tides) occur at times when the Moon is at a right angle to the Sun and the Earth.

# Coastlines

- **A coast** is a continuous stretch of land that borders an ocean. The outline of the coast is called a coastline.

- **The features of a coast** depend on the landscape and weather of that area.

- **Hard rocks** withstand the waves and erode slowly, forming headlands.

- **Wave power** is responsible for the formation of structures such as cliffs, headlands and caves.

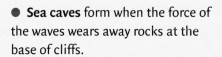

▶ *Waves can create amazing shapes such as pillars called sea stacks.*

- **A cliff is formed** by the pounding of waves on weak spots on the rock face.

- **When rocks at the base of a cliff erode**, they collapse onto the shore and break into tiny fragments, which gradually form wide beaches between the cliff and the ocean. This saves the cliff from further erosion.

- **Continuous erosion** leads to the creation of hollows (sea caves). Sometimes waves pound the headland from both sides, causing two caves to form back-to-back.

- **When two caves meet**, a sea arch forms. The top of the arch links the headland to the mainland.

- **After years of erosion**, sea arches cave in, leaving a column of rock in the sea. This is known as a sea stack.

- **The best-known natural structure** formed by waves is the beach. Waves lose much of their power in shallow waters and instead of eroding they deposit sand and shingle on the coast. These deposits eventually become the beach.

# Sea caves

- **Sea caves** form when the force of the waves wears away rocks at the base of cliffs.

- **Even vein-like cracks** in a rock are enough to cause it to crumble under continuous pounding by waves.

- **Waves penetrate cracks** in a rock and exert high pressure, forcing the rocks to crumble from within, forming small hollows.

- **These hollows** expand further when sand, gravel and rocks brought by the waves start eroding the inner walls.

- **Some sea caves** are submerged in water during high tide, and can be seen only when the water recedes.

- **Sea caves are an attraction** for adventurers and tourists. They can be explored in small boats or on foot when the water level is low.

- **Sea caves are common** on the Pacific coasts of the United States and in the Greek islands.

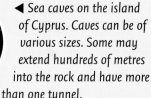

◀ *Sea caves on the island of Cyprus. Caves can be of various sizes. Some may extend hundreds of metres into the rock and have more than one tunnel.*

- **The Blue Grotto of Capri** in Italy is famous for the bluish glow of its waters. This glow is caused by sunlight pouring through an underwater hole. The light shines on the water to create a brilliant blue glow.

- **Sea caves are full of marine life.** Sea anemones, sponges and starfish are found in the bigger caves.

> ★ STAR FACT ★
> One of the largest known sea caves is the Painted Cave on Santa Cruz Island off California. It is nearly 375 m long.

# Volcanic oceans

● **Almost 90 percent** of the world's volcanic activity takes place under the ocean. Most undersea volcanoes are along the mid-ocean ridge.

● **The Pacific Ocean** contains more than 80 percent of the world's active volcanoes. They encircle the ocean along the continent margins to form the 'Ring of Fire'.

● **Volcanoes are formed** when two tectonic plates drift apart and hot molten rock called magma oozes out. They are also formed if one plate crashes into another.

● **When the lava** oozing out of an underwater volcano comes into contact with water, it solidifies, often forming round lumps called pillow lava. Several tiny marine organisms thrive on these lumps of lava.

● **Hot springs** (hydrothermal vents) are also found on the sea floor along the mid-ocean ridge. They are formed when water seeps into the crust as two plates pull apart. This water is heated by the magma and shoots up through cracks in the ocean floor.

● **The temperature of water** in and around a vent can go up to 400° C. It is rich in minerals and the gas hydrogen sulphide.

★ STAR FACT ★
Mauna Kea and Mauna Loa in Hawaii are the tallest volcanic mountains on Earth. Measured from its base on the ocean floor, Mauna Kea is taller than even Mount Everest, at 9800 m.

● **The scalding water** mixes with the surrounding cold water to create jets of warm water. These are often black because of the mineral content in the water, so they are also called black smokers.

● **Hydrothermal vents** were first discovered in 1977 near the Galapagos Islands along the eastern Pacific Ocean basin.

● **The water at the deep-ocean floor** is too cold for creatures to survive, but hydrothermal vents are like underwater oases. Long tubeworms and other life forms that are not found anywhere else in the world thrive near these vents.

▼ *Hydrothermal vents are home to rat tail fish and sea spiders as well as giant tube worms.*

Key

1   Rat tail fish

2   Hydrothermal vents

3   Sea spider

4   Tube worms

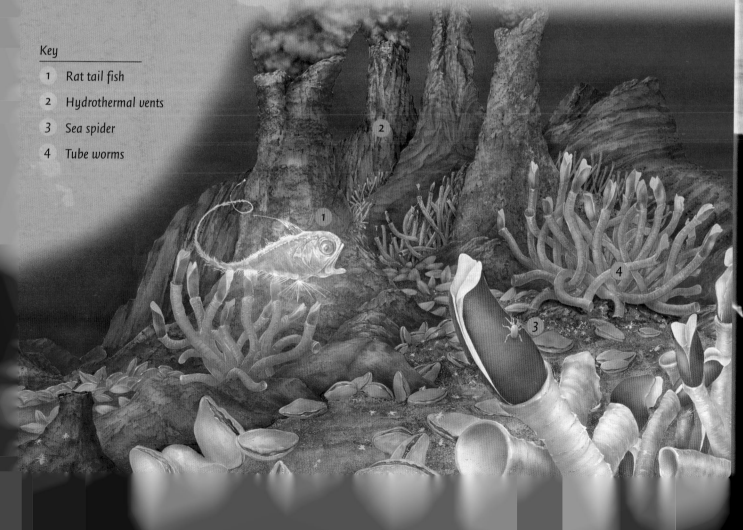

# Volcanic islands

- **Undersea volcanoes** often lead to the formation of volcanic islands. Some are formed around one or two volcanic vents, others can be made up of a series of vents.

1    2    3

▲ (1) Molten rock breaks through Earth's crust . (2) More lava is deposited on the seabed, so a cone shape builds up. (3) When this breaks the water's surface, a new island appears.

- **Volcanic activity** often occurs at the point between two tectonic plates.

- **Sometimes, volcanoes are formed** away from the plate boundaries near fixed points of volcanic activity located beneath tectonic plates (hot spots).

- **Molten magma** from deep within the mantle forces its way through fissures (gaps) in the plate and flow out to form seamounts.

- **Over millions of years** magma oozes out of these seamounts, which gradually rise above the ocean surface as islands. These islands are called oceanic high islands.

- **Volcanic activity** on an island ceases when it is carried away from the hotspot when the tectonic plates move.

- **Then another island is created** at the hotspot. This continues until a chain of islands, such as the Hawaiian Islands, is created.

- **The hot spot** in the Pacific Ocean is currently under the Big Island – the largest among the Hawaiian Islands.

- **Iceland was formed** by volcano activity near the ocean ridge. It is the only part of the mid-oceanic ridge that emerges from the surface.

- **Some volcanic islands** are formed in the shape of arcs, such as Marianas in the Pacific Ocean.

# The angry oceans

- **The oceans** can wreak havoc in the form of tsunamis, whirlpools and hurricanes.

- **Tsunamis are massive waves** generated in the oceans by certain natural disturbances. They lash against the shore with a great force can can cause a lot of damage.

- **Most often created by earthquakes**, tsunamis can also be generated by landslides and undersea volcanic eruptions.

- **Most tsunamis** originate along an earthquake-prone zone known as the Ring of Fire, around the Pacific Ocean.

◀ Hurricanes can cause devastation if they reach the coast.

**★ STAR FACT ★**
El Niño was first observed by fishermen in South America, who noticed that this phenomenon usually occurred around Christmas.

- **'Tsunami' is a Japanese word** meaning 'harbour wave'.

- **Hurricanes are cyclones** arising in the tropical or sub-tropical waters.

- **A whirlpool** is created when opposing currents meet. Most whirlpools are not dangerous, but some are powerful enough to destroy small boats.

- **Moskstraumen** off the coast of Norway and Old Sow near Deer Island in Canada are two of the world's most powerful whirlpools.

- **El Niño** is another interesting oceanic phenomenon that has a considerable effect on the global weather. It is the warming of surface waters in the eastern Pacific Ocean, near the Equator.

# Coral reefs

● **Coral reefs** are formed by colonies of coral polyps – tiny animals that use minerals in the sea to produce their protective outer skeletons. These skeletons form hard and branching structures called coral reefs.

● **Coral polyps eat algae.** They also use their tentacles to capture tiny creatures called zooplankton.

● **Corals are ancient animals** that have been around for 250 millions years.

● **Coral reefs are home** to numerous sea animals. Starfish, reef sharks, sponges, crabs, lobsters, anemones and a huge variety of fish add to the colour of coral reefs.

● **Coral reefs are found** in warm and shallow waters, usually within 30 degrees north and south of the Equator.

Key

1. Parrot fish
2. Giant clam
3. Clown fish
4. Cleaner wrasse fish
5. Lion fish

● **There are three kinds of coral reefs.** These are fringing and barrier reefs, and coral atolls.

● **Fringing reefs extend** from the land into the sea. Barrier reefs are found further from the shore, separated from the mainland by a lagoon. Atolls are ring-shaped formations of coral islands, around a lagoon.

● **The Great Barrier Reef** in the Coral Sea off the north-eastern coast of Australia is the biggest of all coral reefs. It is over 2000 km long.

● **Coral reefs are also found** in the Indian Ocean and the Red Sea. Some of them also stretch along the Atlantic Ocean from Florida in the United States to the Caribbean Sea and Brazil.

● **Coral reefs, especially the Great Barrier Reef**, are major tourist attractions because of their fascinating structures, vibrant colours and rich marine life.

● **The stinging hydroid coral** found in the Indian and Pacific oceans uses special chemicals to paralyse plankton, which forms a major part of its diet.

▼ A single coral reef may be home to as many as 3000 species of living things.

# Amazing corals

- **An atoll** is a coral reef surrounding a lagoon. The formation of atolls can take millions of years.

- **Atoll formation** begins with the creation of a coral reef around a volcanic island. Wind and waves erode the island and it begins to sink. The reef grows upwards to form a barrier separated from the island by a lagoon. At this stage these islands are called barrier reef islands.

- **The barrier reef islands** continue to sink until they are submerged. The reef around the island continues to grow upwards to form a ring surrounding a lagoon. This is called a coral atoll.

- **Coral atolls are formed** mostly in the warm, shallow waters of the Indian and Pacific oceans

- **Sometimes, waves and wind** deposit pieces of coral and sand on top of reefs. Over time, this debris piles up to form low-lying islands called cays.

- **Coral cays** support a variety of plant and animal life. Some eventually become small islands that people live on.

▶ *Coral reefs are the largest ecosystems on our planet.*

- **Other cays** move across the reef and even disappear with time.

- **Kiritimati**, or Christmas Island, is the largest coral atoll in the world.

- **The Belize atolls** are unique because they developed on non-volcanic ridges.

- **The colourful reefs** that surround coral islands are home to beautiful and exotic marine creatures. These reefs have become popular destinations for undersea diving.

# Icy water

- **The oceans** close to the North and South poles – the Arctic and the Antarctic – are partly frozen throughout the year.

- **These oceans** are covered with dazzling white icebergs and huge sheets of floating ice, which make it difficult for ships to navigate these waters.

- **The Antarctic Ocean** surrounds Antarctica, which is an island continent. The Arctic Ocean surrounds the North Pole.

- **In winter** the water close to the land is frozen. The ice melts in the summer and large chunks of ice, called icebergs, break off and float in the sea.

- **Massive slabs of permanent ice**, or ice shelves, break off and also float close to the shores in the Antarctic Ocean. The Ross Ice Shelf is the largest of these.

◀ *The term 'iceberg' has its origin in the German word 'berg', meaning mountain.*

- **Unlike the South Pole**, there is no land mass around the North Pole. Most parts of the Arctic Ocean are covered by ice sheets.

- **Other seas that freeze in the winter** include the Okhotsk Sea and the Bering Sea.

- **The water in the Polar Regions** might be freezing cold, but it is still home to a huge variety of marine life. Whales, sharks, jellyfish, squid, seals, polar bears and seabirds can be found living in and around these oceans.

- **The harsh climate on the Antarctic continent** is not conducive to life. This region is largely uninhabited. Only scientists brave the cold to conduct research. However, Inuit are known to live in the Arctic region.

# The Arctic

- **The Arctic Circle** is the imaginary circle surrounding the North Pole. It is not a single land mass. All of the Earth that falls inside the circle is termed as 'the Arctic'.

- **The North Pole** is in the middle of the Arctic Ocean. The ocean is surrounded by Russia, Greenland, Iceland, Canada and Alaska.

- **The coldest part of the Arctic region** is Oymyakon in Siberia, with a temperature of –68° C.

- **The tundra is the extremely cold land** surrounding the Arctic Ocean.

- **The Arctic tundra** is so cold that the ground beneath the surface remains frozen all year. This frozen ground is called permafrost.

- **The permafrost** prevents plants growing deep roots, but a variety of mosses, shrubs and small flowering plants can be found.

- **The Arctic is home** to animals such as the Arctic fox, seals, orcas, polar bears and caribou.

- **Inuit** were the first human inhabitants of the Arctic.

- **Traditionally the Inuit** depended on seals for their survival. During summer they travelled in boats made from animal skin, called kayaks. In winter they used dog sledges.

- **Today most Inuit** live in houses made of wood. They wear modern clothing and travel in motorboats or snowmobiles. They also speak English, Russian or Danish as well as their native tongue.

▼ *Snowmobiles have replaced dog sledges as a popular mode of transport in the Arctic region.*

# Antarctica

- **Antarctica** lies in the southernmost point of the globe, surrounding the South Pole.

- **The total area** of Antarctica is about 14 million sq km in summer.

- **Antarctica is roughly round** in shape. Two seas cut into the continent. It is surrounded by the Antarctic Ocean.

- **Antarctica was the last** continent to be discovered.

- **This continent has the lowest temperatures** on Earth. During winter, the temperature falls below –90 °C.

- **Antarctica receives no rainfall**. The snow hardly melts or evaporates. Instead, it accumulates in icy layers.

> ★ **STAR FACT** ★
> The Antarctic Treaty (1961) allows only peaceful activities such as scientific research on the continent and its ocean.

- **The ice that covers Antarctica** makes up 70 percent of the Earth's fresh water.

- **The continent is divided** into Greater and West Antarctica. These areas are separated by the Transantarctic Mountains, most of which are buried under ice.

- **At certain places** taller parts of the Transantarctic Mountains emerge from the ice. These tips of rocks (nunatak) are often home to birds, such as snow petrels.

◄ *Antarctica has been covered with ice for about five million years.*

# Glaciers and icebergs

★ **STAR FACT** ★

The part of an iceberg that is visible above water is only a small portion of its entire bulk. The enormous submerged part is very dangerous to ships.

● **Glaciers** are moving masses of ice. They form on top of high mountains and in the polar regions.

● **Once the glacier attains enough weight**, it starts sliding down a slope.

● **Glaciers can be divided** into four types – icecap, alpine, piedmont and continental glaciers.

● **Alpine glaciers originate** from mountains and feed mountain rivers.

● **Piedmont glaciers** are formed when alpine glaciers join at the foot of a mountain.

● **A huge blanket of ice and snow** covers most of Greenland and Antarctica. These formations are known as continental glaciers, or ice sheets.

● **Icecap glaciers** are smaller versions of continental glaciers. They often occupy elevated regions. Sometimes they break off at the edges and fall into the ocean.

● **Icebergs are huge chunks of ice** that break off the ends of ice sheets, glaciers and ice caps and float into the sea.

● **The ice in some icebergs** contains tiny air bubbles that reflect light and give the iceberg a dazzling look.

● **Icebergs are different shapes and sizes**. They can be broadly classified as rounded, irregular and tabular, or resembling a table top.

▼ *The process by which icebergs break away from glaciers is called 'calving'.*

# Early marine life

● **It is believed** that life on Earth originated in the oceans around 3.8 billion years ago.

● **Some scientists think** lightning strikes triggered a reaction among certain compounds and gases in the atmosphere, which may have led to the formation of proteins and enzymes.

● **The proteins and enzymes** rained down on the oceans and developed into primitive single-celled organisms.

● **Around 620 million years ago**, soft-bodied multi-cellular life-forms appeared for the first time.

● **Some of the earliest creatures** looked like modern jellyfish. They were very small and had a variety of shapes.

● **These early animals** evolved into more complex life-forms that are recognized today, including sponges, jellyfish, corals, flatworms and molluscs.

◄ *Coelacanths have hardly changed over millions of years.*

● **The earliest fish** appeared around 480 million years ago. The modern hagfish and lamprey are the only surviving members of this group.

● **Around 450 million years ago**, sharks and bony fish began to evolve. The first bony fish were small and had armoured plates for defence.

● **Early bony fish** were either ray-finned or lobe-finned. The coelacanth and the modern lungfish are the only lobe-finned fish that survive today.

● **Most scientists believe** that lobe-finned fish used their fins to come out of the water for very short periods. This led to the evolution of amphibians, which themselves eventually evolved into other land creatures.

# Modern marine life

● **The first modern fish** appeared around 250 million years ago. The ancient ray-finned fish gave rise to the neopterygians, which are considered to be the ancestors of the modern fish.

● **The oceans of the modern world** are no different from the primitive oceans in terms of the number of creatures that live there. Today, the oceans are home to several species of mammals and reptiles, numerous small creatures and more than 20,000 species of fish.

● **Oceans are divided into two regions** – the benthic zone, or the ocean floor, and the pelagic zone, which is the vast expanse of water.

● **The pelagic zone** is further divided into three zones. The topmost zone, called the epipelagic zone, supports around 90 percent of marine life.

● **The epipelagic zone** is the only ocean zone that gets sunlight. Apart from plants, many species of fish, reptiles and mammals dwell here.

● **The twilight zone** is just below the epipelagic zone. Very little sunlight reaches this zone, making it impossible for plants to survive here. However, deep sea fish are found in this zone.

● **Some animals** living in the twilight zone are bioluminescent. Special organs, called photophores, in the bodies of these animals give off a greenish light.

● **The midnight zone** is the lowest zone and is completely dark and extremely cold. Very few creatures live in this zone and most of them do not have eyes.

● **Oceans are advanced ecosystems**. Tiny plants and animals, called plankton, float on the surface and form the base of the oceanic food chain.

● **Many land creatures** depend on oceans for survival. These include seabirds, and animals such as polar bears. They feed on fish that swim close to the surface.

▼ Oceans are home to nearly 300,000 different living species, ranging from huge whales to tiny fish.

# Fish facts

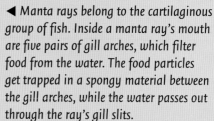

- **Fish are vertebrates**, so they have a backbone. They live in water, breathe through their gills and have scales.

- **Fish are found in varied habitats** – from the deepest oceans to the smallest streams.

- **Most fish live in oceans**. Only one in five lives in fresh water.

- **Unlike mammals**, fish are cold-blooded. Their body temperature changes with their surroundings.

- **Fish are broadly divided** into two main groups – jawed and jawless. Jawless fish, such as lamprey and hagfish, have a sucker-like mouth with horny teeth.

- **Jawed fish** are further divided into cartilaginous and bony fish. The skeleton of cartilaginous fish is made of tissue called cartilage. Sharks, rays and chimaeras are cartilaginous fish.

◄ *Manta rays belong to the cartilaginous group of fish. Inside a manta ray's mouth are five pairs of gill arches, which filter food from the water. The food particles get trapped in a spongy material between the gill arches, while the water passes out through the ray's gill slits.*

- **The skeletons of bony fish** are made of bone. They are the most common of all fish species. Most of them have a bladder that helps them to swim.

- **Most fish have a streamlined body** to help them swim. The blue shark is one of the fastest swimming fish.

- **Fish feed on other creatures of the ocean**. The smallest feed on microscopic creatures such as zooplankton. Larger fish prey on smaller marine creatures.

- **Fish are important** to humans as food, since they are a good source of protein. Excessive fishing has endangered some species, while others are already extinct.

# Flying fish

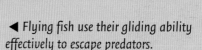

- **Flying fish** do not actually fly. They leap into the air and glide for short distances.

- **The average length** of a flying fish is around 20–30 cm. The California flying fish, found in the Pacific Ocean, is the largest species. It can grow up to a length of 40 cm.

- **The pectoral fins** of flying fish have similar functions to a bird's wings. The two-winged flying fish have very large pectoral fins that they stretch out to soar.

- **Some flying fish** have four 'wings'. In addition to large pectoral fins, these species also have large pelvic fins.

- **When threatened**, flying fish build up speed under the water's surface by thrashing their tails and holding their fins close to the body. The fish then leap into the air and glide for about 20–30 seconds.

◄ *Flying fish use their gliding ability effectively to escape predators.*

- **Flying fish** can leap to a height of 180 cm and cover a distance of over 150 m. In between glides, they return to the water to gain speed.

- **They can glide at double the speed** they swim, and are known to accelerate from 36 km/h in water to 72 km/h in air.

- **The ability to glide** helps flying fish escape from sea predators like tuna and mackerel. But once in the air, they become the target of sea birds.

- **Young flying fish** look very different from their parents. The young ones have whiskers on their lower jaw, which disappear when they mature.

- **Flying fish usually swim in schools**. At times, a whole school leaps into the air and glides together.

# Herring

- **Herring are a family** of marine fish, often found in the waters of the North Atlantic and the North Pacific.

- **Herring feed on small fish** and plankton. They are an important part of the diet of larger creatures such as sharks, seals, whales and seabirds.

- **There are over 360 species** in the herring family, which includes fish such as sardines, anchovies and shad.

- **Sardines get their name** from an island in the Mediterranean, called Sardinia, where the fish were once abundant.

- **In the United States**, 'sardine' is another name for herring. However, the true sardine is the young of the pilchard, found off the Mediterranean and Atlantic coasts.

▶ *It is believed that herring swim in huge schools to increase their chances of survival.*

- **Herrings' bodies** are streamlined, making them excellent swimmers. Most herring, sardines and anchovies are less than 90 cm in length.

- **The Atlantic herring** is the best-known variety. It is thought to be the most common all fishspecies.

- **Atlantic herring are bluish green in colour**, with a silvery underside. The Pacific herring is quite similar to the Atlantic herring.

- **The wolf herring** is the largest of the herring family. It is a fierce hunter and can grow to a length of 3 m.

- **Herring are processed and sold in several forms**. They can be smoked, dried, salted or pickled. Processed herring are sold as kippers, bloaters and red herring.

# Tuna and mackerel

- **Tuna and mackerel** belong to the Scombridae family.

- **Both tuna and mackerel** are fast swimmers. Their torpedo-shaped bodies and crescent tails allow these fish to thrust through the water at great speeds.

- **Mackerel have sleek, shiny bodies** and large mouths. The head does not have any scales.

- **Mackerel are found in cool waters** around the northeast United States, Canada, Great Britain and Norway. They remain close to the water surface and eat small crabs and fish.

- **The Atlantic mackerel** is the most common variety. It is blue and silver in colour and can grow up to half a metre in length.

- **Tuna are found in most parts of the world**. They have a rounded structure and are sleeker than mackerel.

- **Tuna require lots of oxygen**. They swim with their mouths open, shooting jets of water over their gills. The oxygen is extracted from this water.

▲ *A mackerel's back shows a greeny-blue sheen, but its underside is pale, allowing it to camouflage itself and surprise its prey.*

- **Their system of breathing** means that tuna can never remain still.

- **Tuna are not cold-blooded**. They are able to maintain a body temperature a few degrees warmer than the water.

- **Tuna swim in schools** and can travel long distances. They come to coastal areas to lay eggs. The eggs usually hatch within 24 hours.

- **Bluefin tuna are large marine fish**. Adults weigh over 680 kg and can swim at a speed of about 90 km/h.

# Swordfish

- **Swordfish are found** in tropical and temperate waters. They are mostly dark in colour, but have a lighter coloured belly.

- **Swordfish get their name** from their upper jaw, which extends to form a long sword-like snout with a sharp point. This jaw does not have teeth.

- **The snout is used for both defence and attack.** It is believed that swordfish dash into schools of fish to injure or spear prey with the snout.

- **Like marlin and sailfish**, swordfish are good swimmers. They can swim very long distances in pursuit of prey.

- **Swordfish have a crescent-shaped tail** that is characteristic of fast swimmers belonging to the same family. However, unlike marlin, swordfish do not have pelvic fins.

- **Swordfish swim near the surface of the water.** Some species have been known to swim in schools, but most prefer to be alone.

▶ Swordfish prefer to swim in water where ocean currents meet.

- **Swordfish feed on mackerel**, herring and other small fish that swim in schools. Sometimes they dive deep into the ocean in search of sardine.

- **Swordfish can grow over 4 m in length.** Their 'sword' accounts for almost one-third of their length. The jaws of a young swordfish are equal in length. The upper jaw grows longer with age.

- **When attacked**, swordfish can become very violent. It is believed that they can punch holes into small wooden boats. When they are wounded, they thrash about and can cause serious injury.

- **Swordfish is a popular seafood.** The swordfish population has decreased significantly because of overfishing.

# Barracuda

- **Barracuda are powerful predators.** In some coastal regions, they are more feared than sharks.

- **Barracuda have** long heads and slender bodies. They vary from 40 cm to almost 2 m in length.

- **These powerful swimmers** are found in the tropical waters of the Pacific, Atlantic and Indian oceans.

- **The mouth of the barracuda** contains a number of fang-like teeth. These predators have a forked tail, and their dorsal fins are widely separated.

- **The great barracuda**, found in the Pacific and Atlantic oceans, grows to a length of 1.8 m and can weigh as much as 41 kg. Also called the 'tiger of the sea', this aggressive predator is known to attack divers and swimmers.

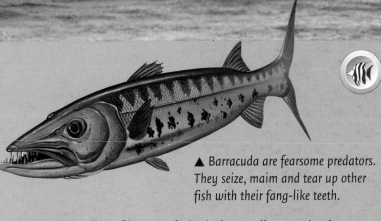

▲ Barracuda are fearsome predators. They seize, maim and tear up other fish with their fang-like teeth.

- **The diet of barracuda** includes sardine, anchovies and squid.

- **Smaller barracuda** swim and hunt in schools, while larger ones hunt alone.

- **Barracuda are often compared with sharks** because of their aggressive nature.

- **Barracuda are guided by their sense of sight** rather than smell. Divers avoid wearing bright costumes that can attract these aggressive fish.

- **Their strength and vigour have made barracuda extremely popular** with anglers. Barracuda usually succeed in escaping from the fish hook, making the sport of game fishing more challenging.

★ STAR FACT ★
The flesh of some barracuda species is poisonous to humans because the fish they feed on are poisonous. The barracuda are immune to this poison.

# Eels

● **Eels are snake-like fish** that live in shallow waters. Most live in the sea, but a few are found in fresh water.

● **Eels are normally found** among coral reefs and on the ocean floor. There are about 690 species of eels. The most common include conger, moray and gulper eels.

● **Most species of eel** are around 1 m long. However, the conger eel can grow up to 3 m in length.

● **A species of moray eel** found in the Pacific Ocean has been known to grow over 3.5 m in length. There are about 100 different species of moray eels.

● **Eels do not have a tail fin**. Their dorsal fin, which runs along the top of the body, provides them with the power to swim.

● **Some eel species** have scales, but the bodies of most eels are covered with a slippery layer of mucus.

● **Eels are graceful swimmers** but are not very fast. Some species, like the American eel, can breathe through their skin and can survive for some time out of water.

● **Gulper eels** live at a depth of almost 1000 m. Since light does not reach these parts of the ocean, they have small eyes or none at all. These eels swim with open mouths, ready to gulp down any creature that comes their way.

● **Freshwater eels** travel to the sea to lay eggs. The adults dive deep into the sea to breed and then die.

● **The eggs of freshwater eels** hatch into leaf-shaped larvae that drift about for almost four years. Once they mature, the young eels, called elvers, swim back to the rivers, where they live until it is time for them to breed.

▼ *There are more than 600 species of eels that are broadly divided into 19 families. Of these, 18 live in the oceans, while one spends part of its life in fresh water.*

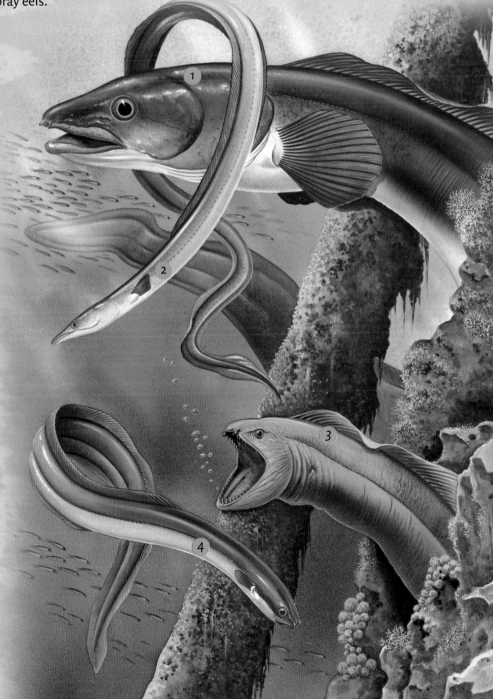

**Key**

1. Conger
2. Snake eel
3. Green moray
4. European eel

# Seahorses

● **Seahorses are tiny creatures.** They get their name from their horse-shaped heads.

● **The size of a seahorse** ranges from less than a centimetre to about 13 cm. The common seahorse, found in the northern Atlantic Ocean, is the largest species.

● **Seahorses have a long mouth** with tubular jaws and an elongated tail. Their only similarity to fish is the dorsal fin.

● **Seahorses use their curly tails** to attach themselves to coral branches and seaweeds. They swim very slowly by flapping their dorsal fin.

● **Seahorses live close** to seashores across the world. They eat small fish and plankton by swallowing them whole.

● **Instead of scales,** seahorses have a series of large rectangular bony plates. These plates protect them from predators, such as crabs.

◀ *Seahorses are often vibrantly coloured and are usually found swimming among coral reefs.*

● **The pencil-shaped pipefish** belongs to the same family as the seahorse. It can grow up to a length of about 50 cm.

● **The seahorse family** consists of over 270 species. Others in this family include seadragons, shrimpfish, sea moths and trumpetfish.

● **A female lays eggs** in a pouch on the male's body. The male carries the eggs while they hatch and until the young seahorses are able to swim out through an opening in the pouch.

● **The Chinese use seahorses** to make traditional medicines. Seahorses are also valued as aquarium pets because of their unique shape and colours.

# Sharks

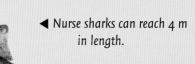

● **Sharks** belong to the cartilaginous group of fish. There are over 350 species of sharks.

● **Sharks are found** in oceans across the world. Some sharks can also survive in fresh water.

● **Most sharks have torpedo-shaped bodies.** They also have large tail fins that give them extra power.

● **A shark's skin** is not covered with smooth scales like bony fish. Instead, its skin is covered with tiny, tooth-like structures called dermal denticles that give the skin a sandpaper-like quality.

● **Sharks are the primary predators,** or hunters, of the ocean. They have special abilities to locate prey. The great white shark, the most feared predator of all, can smell a drop of blood in 100 l of water.

● **The whale shark** is the largest fish. It can grow up to 14 m in length. However, some species, like the spined pygmy shark, are no more than 20 cm long.

◀ *Nurse sharks can reach 4 m in length.*

● **There are different shapes of shark.** Hammerheads have a T-shaped head, which helps them make sharp turns. Reef-dwelling sharks have a flat body.

● **The diet of sharks** includes seals, squid, fish and other marine creatures. Some sharks, like the whale shark and the basking shark, eat plankton and small fish.

● **Depending upon their diet,** sharks have different kinds of teeth. Some, like the great white and tiger sharks, have sharp pointed teeth that help them tear into their prey.

● **Certain species,** like the reef sharks, have flat plate-like teeth that can crush the hard shells of the animals they eat.

# Incredible hunters

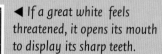

- **Sharks are the best hunters** in the ocean. They have strong senses that help them hunt and travel great distances.

- **A shark's teeth** are its most powerful weapon. A shark can have as many as 3000 teeth, in three rows.

- **It is thought** that almost one-third of a shark's brain is devoted to detecting smell.

- **Some sharks** have whisker-like projections on their snouts (nasal barbels).to help them feel for prey.

- **Sharks also have good eyesight**. Most of them hunt at night and have enhanced night vision

- **Sharks ears are inside their head**. Each ear leads to a small sensory pore on the shark's head.

- **It is believed that sharks** can hear over a distance of 250 m, and detect sounds in the frequency of 25–100 Hz.

◄ *If a great white feels threatened, it opens its mouth to display its sharp teeth.*

- **Sharks have an extra sense organ** known as the 'lateral line'. This is a tube that runs down each side of a shark's body, under the skin.

- **As a shark swims**, ripples pass into the lateral line through its skin. Tiny hairs inside the lateral line sense the ripples and send signals to the shark's brain.

> ★ STAR FACT ★
> Some sharks have special eyelids called nictitating membranes. These close when the shark is about to bite, to protect the eyes from being damaged.

# Great white shark

- **The great white** is the largest predatory shark. It has a pointed snout and a large tail fin.

- **Commonly found** in temperate waters, great white sharks are grey in colour, with a white underbelly.

- **One of the biggest of all sharks**, the great white is normally about 4.5 m in length, but it is thought that some grow as long as 6 m.

- **The teeth** of great whites have saw-like ( serrated) edges, and can grow up to 7.5 cm long.

- **The diet of this shark** includes sea lions, seals and sea turtles. Young great whites eat fish, rays and small sharks.

- **Great whites** do not chew their food. They use their sharp teeth to rip the prey into small pieces that are then swallowed whole.

> ★ STAR FACT ★
> Although it has a reputation as a man-eater, the great white has been responsible for only 58 deaths since 1876!

- **The great white usually approaches prey** from below. Sometimes they will jump out of water. This is called breaching.

- **Without a swim bladder to keep them afloat** great whites have to swim continuously or they will sink.

- **The eggs of the great white** remain inside the female's body until they hatch. The shark then gives birth to live young.

◄ *Being inside a diving cage is a safe way of observing this most dangerous of shark species.*

# Hammerhead shark

● **Hammerhead sharks** have a wide hammer-shaped head. Their eyes are located on either side of this T-shaped head.

● **The head contains tiny receptors** that detect the prey. Its unusual shape also helps the shark to take sharp turns.

● **The hammerhead is common** in tropical and temperate waters. It is grey or brown in colour, with an off-white belly. This shark migrates towards warmer waters near the Equator in winter.

● **The first dorsal fin of the hammerhead**, which is located on its back, is large and pointed. Like most sharks, it can be seen cutting through the water surface, as the hammerhead cruises along.

● **The great hammerhead is the largest** in the hammerhead family. It can measure up to 4 m in length. Bonnethead sharks are smaller and have a shovel-like head.

● **Hammerhead sharks normally feed on fish**, smaller sharks, squid and octopuses. Stingrays, however, are their favourite food.

● **The great hammerhead is an excellent hunter**. It uses its highly developed senses of smell and direction to track prey.

● **Large teeth** enable the great hammerhead to bite big chunks off its prey.

● **Other varieties of hammerhead sharks** include the scalloped and the smooth hammerhead. Both types are found in moderately temperate waters.

● **Most hammerheads are harmless**, but the great hammerhead is one of the few dangerous species. It is known to have attacked humans.

▼ A scalloped hammerhead shark cruises across a coral reef – an underwater structure built by tiny creatures called coral polyps.

# Whale shark

- **Although they are the largest fish in the world**, whale sharks are not aggressive and pose no threat to humans.

- **Whale sharks live** in warm, tropical waters.

- **The average length of a whale shark** is about 14 m, but some have been known to grow to over 18 m in length.

- **These gentle giants** are very heavy. An average adult whale shark weighs about 15 tonnes. Owing to their size, these sharks cannot move fast. They swim by moving their bodies from side to side.

- **Grey or brown in colour** with an off-white underside, the whale shark has white dots and lines on its back.

- **The mouth of the whale shark** is extremely large and can be as wide as 1.4 m. They have around 300 rows of tiny, hook-like teeth in each jaw.

- **As they swim along** with their mouths open, whale sharks suck in water. Bristles on their gills filter their tiny prey, while water passes out through the gill slits.

▼ *The patterns on a whale shark's body help it blend into its surroundings.*

- **The diet of whale sharks** consists mainly of plankton, sardines, krill and anchovies.

- **Whale sharks** are known to wait for hours at breeding grounds to capture freshly laid fish eggs to eat.

- **Although whale sharks** are usually solitary, they have been observed swimming in schools.

# Rays

▶ *The spotted eagle ray is identified by the spots on its back, which can be white, yellow or green in colour.*

- **Rays are cartilaginous fish.** Their skeletons are made of cartilage.

- **Sharks and chimaeras** (ratfish) belong to the same group of fish as rays.

- **Rays are found in oceans** across the world. Most live near the seabed. They bury themselves in the sand when threatened.

- **These fish have broad, flat bodies**chimera Their eyes are located on the upper surface of the body, while the mouth and gills are on the lower side.

- **Rays are usually brown or black** in colour, with a light underside. Some species can change their colour to match the surroundings.

- **Some species are less than 10 cm** in width, while others measure over 6 m across.

- **The pectoral fins of rays** are located behind their heads. These huge fins stretch from both sides of the head to the tail. The ray uses its 'wings' to swim through the water.

- **Rays' tails vary** in size and structure. Most rays have a long tail, but some have a short one. Rays use their tail as a rudder while swimming and also to defend themselves.

- **Different species of rays** have different forms of defence. The long, whip-like tail of the stingray has sharp spines that inject poison into prey.

- **Most species of rays** feed on crustaceans, such as crabs, krill and shrimps. The manta ray prefers to eat plankton.

★ STAR FACT ★
The electric ray has a pair of electric organs behind its head, which can give powerful shocks measuring up to 200 volts. These shocks can stun or kill prey.

# Whales

- **Whales are among the largest** and heaviest animals on Earth. Their size can range from 2 m to over 30 m.

- **Being mammals**, whales do not have gills. The nostrils of whales (blowholes) are located on top of the head.

- **Whales hold their breath underwater**. They come up to the surface and open their blowholes to breathe. After taking in the air, they dive into the water again. Their blowholes remain closed underwater.

- **The spout** (blow) that can be seen rising from the blowhole is stale air that condenses and vaporizes the moment it is released into the atmosphere.

- **Whales are divided** into two main groups: toothed whales and baleen whales. Together, these groups contain 81 known species.

- **Toothed whales** have small teeth, which they use to kill prey such as squid. This group includes dolphins, killer whales, sperm whales, beluga whales and porpoises.

- **Toothed whales emit sound waves** that are bounced off an object, revealing its size, shape and location. This is known as echolocation.

- **Toothed whales use echolocation** to distinguish between prey and non-prey objects.

- **Baleen whales** are toothless. They trap prey in sieve-like structures hanging from their upper jaws.

- **Baleen whales are also known as** great whales. This group includes grey, humpback and the blue whale.

◀ *The tails of whales have wide flukes, which move up and down to power them through water.*

# Baleen and blubber

- **A baleen whale's** huge mouth contains rows of baleen plates. These plates have fringed edges that filter plankton from the water.

- **Whales of this group** swim with their mouths open and take in water containing krill and other small creatures. These get trapped in the baleen. The whale licks the food off the baleen and swallows it.

- **Baleen was once valued** for its plastic-like qualities, and great whales were widely hunted as a result. The demand for baleen has now diminished.

- **Whales have a thick layer of fat**, called blubber, between the skin and the flesh that preserves body heat.

- **Blubber helps** to keep the animals afloat and is a source of stored energy.

◀ *Humpback whales, like all baleen whales, are filter feeders.*

- **Toothed whales** have smaller mouths than great whales. Their teeth are uniform in size and shape.

- **Most whales swim and feed** in groups called pods.

- **Whales sometimes** pop their head above the surface and float motionless. This is known as 'logging'.

- **Some whales** are acrobatic and can leap out of the water. This is known as 'breaching'.

- **Some whales also lift their heads** vertically out of the water before slipping back below. This is known as 'spyhopping'. It is believed that they do this to obtain a view above the surface.

# Blue whale

▶ Blue whale calves feed on their mother's rich milk until they are around eight months old.

● **Blue whales** are the largest creatures to have ever lived on this planet.

● **Their average length** is 25 m but some can grow to more than 30 m.

● **These whales are blue-grey in colour** with light patches on the back.

● **The body is streamlined** with a large tail fin. The dorsal fin is small, while the tail is thick and large. Blue whales have splashguards in front of their two blowholes.

● **Blue whales** are migratory animals. They live near the tropics during winter and migrate towards icy waters in summer.

● **The diet of a blue whale** consists of small fish, plankton and krill in enormous quantities. They can eat over 4 tonnes of krill every day.

● **Blue whales** have been known to gather in groups of 60 or more. However, they are largely solitary animals.

● **The spout of a blue whale** is vertical and can be 10–12 m high.

● **Blue whales** are relatively slow swimmers. However, when threatened, these animals can swim at a speed of over 30 km/h.

● **Merciless hunting** over several decades has caused the blue whale population to decline drastically. It is currently an endangered species, and only 5000 are thought to exist worldwide.

# Killer whale

▶ The offspring of killer whales may stay together for 10 to 20 years.

● **Despite their name**, killer whales, also known as orcas, are the largest members of the dolphin family.

● **They have a black body** with white patches on their underside and behind each eye.

● **Found in oceans** across the world, killer whales prefer to live in colder waters. They do not migrate in summer like great whales, and often live close to the coast.

● **The average length** of the killer whale is 8–10 m. They have sharp, hooked teeth, which they use to rip their prey apart.

● **It is believed the name** 'killer whale' might have been derived from the name 'whale killer', a name given to these animals by 18th century whalers who saw them feeding on other whales and dolphins.

● **The diet of killer whales** is varied. They largely prey on fish, squid, sharks and warm-blooded animals such as seals, seabirds and larger whales.

● **Killer whales** are known as the 'wolves of the sea'. Like wolves, they hunt in groups and hence are able to tackle prey of all shapes and sizes.

● **The pods of killer whales** are divided into resident and transient pods.

● **Resident pods** can consist of 5–50 members who communicate frequently using whistles and high-pitched screams.

● **Transient pods** have a maximum of seven members who feed mainly on marine mammals. Members of transient pods do not communicate frequently with each other.

# Humpback whale

- **Humpback whales** are large baleen whales. They are one of the most active whales and can often be seen leaping out of the water.

- **Found in most parts of the world**, humpback whales migrate to icy waters in the north and south during the summer. In winter, they breed in tropical waters.

- **Humpbacks have a flat head** that has fleshy bumps (tubercles). The body is dark, with white patches. The underside is off-white.

- **The humpback grows up to 15 m in length**. They are named after a hump on which the whale's dorsal fin is located.

- **The tail fin** measures nearly 5.5 m across and has black and white patterns. Each of these patterns is unique, so scientists use them to identify and monitor humpbacks.

- **Humpbacks feed on shrimps**, krill and small fish. They have various methods of feeding.

- **When lunge-feeding**, the humpback opens its mouth wide and swims through a group of prey.

- **When tail-flicking**, the whale lies with its belly just below the surface using its tail to flick prey into its mouth.

- **Bubble-netting** is the most spectacular feeding habit. The humpback slaps its flippers around a school of fish, to create a wall of bubbles, forcing the fish to move to the surface, which makes them easy prey.

- **Male humpbacks** are known for their unusual songs. The sounds vary from squeaks to deep wails. They are usually heard during the breeding season.

◄ Humpbacks have lots of lumps and bumps on their heads called tubercles. Hard-shelled sea creatures called barnacles also live on the whale.

# Beluga

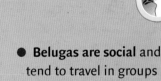

▶ Belugas have a stout body, a small beak and a prominent forehead, which is called a 'melon'.

- **Beluga whales** have a playful nature and this, along with their unusual colour, makes them popular attractions in aquariums.

- **Related to dolphins**, the adult beluga whale is milky white in colour.

- **The colour of the whale** matches its habitat, in the icy Arctic Ocean. Young belugas are grey in colour.

- **Belugas have narrow necks**, and can nod and shake their heads from side to side.

- **Delphinapterus leucas**, the beluga's scientific name means 'white dolphin without wings', referring to the absence of a dorsal fin.

- **The beluga's diet** consists of crab, squid, shrimp and fish. They use their teeth to grab prey rather than to chew.

- **Belugas are social** and tend to travel in groups of 5–20 members, usually led by a single male. During migrations, the groups can exceed 10,000 members.

- **These whales emit various sounds**, from whistles to chirps and squeaks. They are the most vocal whales, earning them the nickname of sea canaries.

- **Belugas are hunted by killer whales**. The young are often killed by polar bears. It is not uncommon to find adult belugas bearing scars from polar bear attacks.

> ★ **STAR FACT** ★
> Belugas do not have a dorsal fin, which
> makes swimming under ice much easier.

# Dolphins

● **Dolphins are close relatives of whales** and form a large part of the toothed whales group. They have a beak-shaped snout and are extremely active and playful.

● **They are found in all oceans**, and are powerful swimmers. The shape of their body and their big flippers help in rapid movement. Dolphins are often spotted riding on waves, probably to conserve energy.

● **Dolphins are good at diving deep** into the ocean and also leaping into the air. Many of them can leap as high as 7 m. They can even turn somersaults before landing into the water with a splash.

● **Like baleen whales**, dolphins have blowholes on top of their head. They surface every two minutes to breathe, before diving under again.

● **Dolphins use echolocation** to hunt and navigate through cloudy waters. They emit a series of high-pitched sound pulses, which bounce off prey or obstacles, enabling dolphins to locate them.

● **These animals hunt in groups**. They chase their prey, surround it, and catch it with their powerful jaws. Dolphins have numerous conical teeth.

● **The smallest dolphin is the tucuxi dolphin**, which is hardly 1 m long. Bottlenose dolphins can reach a length of over 3.5 m, while common dolphins are about 2.5 m long.

● **The killer whale is the largest member** of the dolphin family. It can reach a length of almost 10 m. Like others in the family, the killer whale is very intelligent and can be trained to do tricks.

● **The playful nature of dolphins** has made them extremely popular, especially with children. They are common sights in sea life centres.

● **Dolphins used to be hunted for their meat and oil.** Until recently, thousands used to die every year by getting caught in fishing nets.

> ★ **STAR FACT** ★
> Some scientists believe that dolphins have a language of their own, heard by humans in the form of whistling sounds. Some even believe that they are able to understand sign language.

▼ *Bottlenose dolphins usually swim at speeds of 5–11 km/h, but sometimes they can exceed 32 km/h.*

# Porpoises

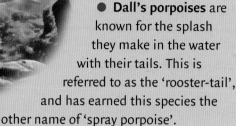

▶ While on the move, the harbour porpoise surfaces six to eight times within a minute. Normally, it can stay under water for about 5 minutes before surfacing again.

- **Porpoises are small**, toothed whales. They are close relatives of dolphins.

- **Usually smaller than dolphins**, porpoises rarely grow to more than 2.2 m. They are grey, blue or black in colour.

- **The dorsal fin of a porpoise** is triangular, whereas the dolphin's is curved. Porpoises do not have a beak.

- **There are several varieties of porpoises**. The harbour (common) porpoise is the best known.

- **Harbour porpoises** are found in cold waters. They have a small body and dorsal fin.

- **There are two varieties of Dall's porpoises** – the dalli type and the truei type. Both are found in the northern Pacific Ocean.

- **Dall's porpoises** are known for the splash they make in the water with their tails. This is referred to as the 'rooster-tail', and has earned this species the other name of 'spray porpoise'.

- **The spectacled porpoise** is found in the South Atlantic. The upper part of its body is bluish black, while the lower half is white.

- **Spectacled porpoises** have black patches around their eyes, which are surrounded by a white line. These resemble spectacles.

- **Burmeister's porpoises** are commonly found off the coasts of South America. It is named after the German biologist Burmeister, who gave this species the scientific name *spinipinnis*, meaning 'spiny fin' due to the blunt structures (tubercles) along the edges of its fins.

# Seals

▶ Seals, such as this leopard seal, are clumsy on land, sliding along the shore with difficulty.

- **Seals are marine mammals**. They belong to the pinnipeds group along with walruses and sea lions. 'Pinniped' means 'fin-footed', as they all have limbs that look like fins.

- **There are two families of seals**: true seals and eared seals. True seals do not have external ear flaps.

- **There are 19 species of true seals**. Eared seals consist of sea lions and fur seals.

- **The limbs of seals** are modified into powerful flippers. Their torpedo-shaped body and their ability to store oxygen, make them great swimmers.

- **The rear flippers** of eared seals are more mobile than those of true seals, and their front flippers are more powerful.

- **Seals spend most of their lives** in water, coming ashore to breed and nurse their young. Some live at sea for months at a time, others return to the shore every day.

- **Most species live in cold regions**, so they have a thick coat of fur as well as a layer of fat (blubber), under their skin, to provides warmth and energy.

- **Seals range in size** from 1–4 m. Galapagos fur seals and ringed seals are the smallest. The largest is the male southern elephant seal, which can grow to 5 m in length.

- **The diet of seals** consists mainly of fish, squid, crabs and shellfish. Leopard seals are among the most aggressive hunters.

- **Killer whales**, sharks and polar bears are the natural predators of seals.

# Sea lions

- **Sea lions are eared seals.** Unlike true seals, they have external ear flaps and their flippers are quite big.

- **These extremely vocal animals** make a roaring noise, which gives them their name. They are brownish in colour, and males being darker than the females.

- **Sea lions use their flippers** to swim and paddle in water as well as walk on land.

- **Being highly social creatures**, sea lions swim in large groups.

- **Steller's sea lion** is the largest type of sea lion – males can grow up to 3 m in length. They are found in the northern waters of the Pacific Ocean.

- **The diet of a sea lion** includes mainly fish, crab, squid, octopus and clams. Steller's sea lion also feed on seals and small otters.

- **Steller's sea lion and California sea lion** are the best-known species. The former are tamed very easily and are popular attractions in water parks.

▶ Sea lions nurse their pups for about a year. During this period they will leave their pups to go hunting in the sea for five days at a time.

- **California sea lions** are found along the rocky western coast of North America. They are also found on the Galapagos Islands. The males are over 2 m in length and the females are smaller.

- **Killer whales** are the biggest enemies of sea lions. Sharks are also known to hunt California sea lions.

- **A large number of sea lions** die as a result of getting caught in fishing nets. There are now laws restricting the hunting of sea lions. Steller's sea lion has been declared as endangered.

# Sea cows

▶ A diver tagging a manatee.

- **Manatees and dugongs are types of sea cow.** They are large, thick-bodied mammals. Other than whales and dolphins, sea cows are the only other mammals that in water.

- **Dugongs are found** in the tropical waters of the Indian and Pacific oceans. Manatees are found off the Caribbean Islands, the southeast United States and West Africa.

- **Sea cows graze on seagrasses** and other aquatic plants. There are only four species in this group, of which three belong to the manatee family.

- **Sea cows are also called sirenians**, after the Sirens (mermaids), of Greek mythology. It is thought that sailors mistook sea cows for creatures that were half human and half fish, thus giving rise to the mermaid legends.

- **Steller's sea cow**, one of the largest species, is now extinct. It was hunted for its meat and skin and the population was completely wiped out.

- **Steller's sea cow was first discovered** in Arctic waters in 1741 by the crew of the Russian explorer, Captain Vitus Bering.

- **Manatees have long, rounded bodies** and their average length is 3.5 m. They are mostly grey in colour.

- **Dugongs and manatees are closely related** to elephants.

- **Manatees and dugongs** are slow swimmers, using their forelimbs and tails to move. They do not have hind limbs.

- **Unlike dugongs**, the manatees' forelimbs are set very close to its head. The tail of the dugong is forked, while the manatee has a round, flat, paddle-like tail.

# Gulls

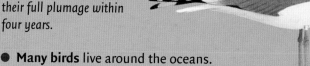

▶ Larger species of gulls, such as the common gull, attain their full plumage within four years.

★ STAR FACT ★
Very few gull species venture into the open seas. Most prefer to keep to the shore, while some come to the coast only during the breeding season.

● **Many birds** live around the oceans. The most common are gulls (seagulls), which are migratory. There are about 43 gull species.

● **Gulls range in length** from 28 cm to 80 cm. Most have white and grey plumage or feathers. Some have black markings on the back, wings and head.

● **Gulls have a sharp, hooked bill**, which helps them kill small birds and other prey. They have webbed feet to paddle on water surfaces, but they cannot dive underwater.

● **Gulls use the wind** to stay aloft without flapping their wings.

● **The colour of the plumage** changes throughout the gull's life, and some have winter and summer plumage.

● **Black-headed gulls** have dark heads and red bills in summer. In winter their heads turn white with a grey spot. It is thought that this gives better camouflage in snow.

● **Many gulls** are great scavengers and feed on dead animal matter along seashores.

● **Gulls are able to fish in shallow waters** and often prey on the eggs of other seabirds.

● **Gulls make simple grass-lined nests**, mostly on flat ground in isolated areas of beaches. Some nest on ledges in cliffs.

● **Commonly found species** include herring, common, black-headed and ring-billed gulls. The great black-backed gull is the largest of all.

# Albatrosses

◀ Once airborne, the graceful albatross can glide for hours without flapping its wings.

● **The albatross** is the largest seabird, weighing about 12 kg. It is commonly found in oceans of the southern hemisphere, but some species also dwell in the North Pacific.

● **Most albatrosses** are white or pale grey in colour, with black wing tips. Some albatrosses have shades of brown.

● **The wandering albatross** has the largest wingspan of all birds, at about 3.7 m. It can grow up to 1.4 m in length, with females being smaller than males.

● **Albatrosses have a sharp bill** with a hooked upper jaw. They also have tubular nostrils and webbed feet. Their long, narrow wings make them powerful gliders.

● **These birds are so heavy** that they have to leap from cliffs to launch into flight.

● **Albatrosses prey on squid**, cuttlefish and small marine creatures.

● **Of all seabirds** albatrosses spend the most time at sea. They even sleep while floating on the surface of the ocean. They come ashore only during the breeding season.

● **Albatrosses nest in colonies** on remote islands. Many have complex mating dances and some change colour during courtship.

● **These birds can travel** thousands of kilometres. Adult albatrosses often go out into the sea in search of food for their young. The parents swallow the prey and regurgitate the food into the chick's mouth when get back to the nest.

● **There is a superstition among sailors** that killing an albatross brings bad luck. This belief forms the theme of Samuel Taylor Coleridge's famous poem *The Rime of the Ancient Mariner*.

# Pelicans

- **Pelicans are easily identified** by their long bill and massive throat pouch. They are the largest diving birds.

- **Adult pelicans** grow up to 1.8 m in length and weigh 4–7 kg. Males are larger than females. Their wing span can measure up to 3 m.

- **There are seven species** of pelican. Most can live near bodies of fresh water, as well as oceans.

- **Most pelicans are white.** Brown and Peruvian pelicans, are dark in colour, and American white pelicans have black wing tips.

- **Pelicans breed in colonies.** Nearly 40,000 birds come together on isolated shores or islands to breed.

- **In some species** the colour of the bill and pouch changes during the mating season.

- **The female pelican** builds a nest by digging a hole in the ground. She lines the hole with grass and feathers. Three days later, she lays her eggs in her new nest.

- **While fishing,** pelicans use their pouch to catch the prey. Once the prey is caught, the pelican draws the pouch close to its chest to empty the water out and swallow the prey.

- **Brown and Peruvian** pelicans dive headlong into the water to catch fish.

- **Most other pelicans** swim and then pounce on their prey. Some fish in groups and drive the fish towards shallow waters where it is easier to capture them. Pelicans feed on small fish and crustaceans.

◀ *The American white pelican does not dive for its food but prefers to fish in large groups.*

# Penguins

- **Penguins are big sea birds** that cannot fly. There are about 17 species, most of which live in the Antarctic region.

- **Some species are found** as far north as the Galapagos Islands. Smaller species are found in warmer waters.

- **Larger penguins are better** at retaining heat, so they can live closer to the South Pole. The emperor penguin is the tallest at 1.2 m. The smallest is the fairy penguin (little blue penguin), at less then 40 cm in height.

- **Penguins have a thick layer of fat** that protects them from the freezing temperatures of the region. Their coats are waterproof.

- **These flightless birds** have black heads and wings, and a white underside. They have sharp bills and a short tail.

▶ *A gentoo penguin and chicks. These social birds live in large groups.*

- **Penguins do not use their wings for flying** – their wings act like flippers that help them swim. Penguins are good divers and can move in water at great speeds.

- **On land,** penguins move clumsily. They are often seen sliding down slopes on their bellies.

- **Adélie penguins** waddle over 300 km every year to reach their breeding grounds. They depend on the Sun to navigate across the ice, so once the sun sets they are at risk of losing their way.

- **Rockhopper penguins** have a tuft of yellow feathers on their head. They are named because they often jump from rock to rock.

- **Penguins have been hunted extensively** by humans for their fat and skin. Their natural enemies are sharks, whales and leopard seals.

# Sea turtles

● **There are only seven species of marine turtles**. They are found in tropical and sub-tropical waters around the world.

● **The leatherback turtle** is the largest sea turtle. The other species are loggerhead, hawksbill, olive ridley, Kemp's ridley, flatback and green sea turtles.

● **A hard shell covers and protects the sea turtle's body**. Compared to the freshwater turtle, the sea turtle has a flatter, less domed shell, which helps it to swim faster.

● **The front limbs of the sea turtle** are larger than the back limbs. These flipper-like limbs help the turtle to 'fly' through the water, although moving on land is quite awkward.

● **The shell of the leatherback sea turtle** is made of a thick, rubbery substance that is strengthened by small bones. These turtles are named after this unusual shell.

● **Sea snakes and sea turtles** are the only reptiles that spend most of their lives in the ocean. The females swim ashore for a few hours each year to lay eggs.

● **Sea turtles prefer to lay their eggs at night**. The female digs a pit in the sand with her flippers. She then lays about 50–150 eggs, and covers the nest with sand.

● **Once the eggs hatch** the young turtles struggle out of their sandpit and make their way to the sea. On the way, many babies fall prey to seabirds, crabs, otters and other predators.

● **The diet of sea turtles** differs from species to species. Leatherbacks prefer jellyfish, while olive ridleys and loggerheads eat hard-shelled creatures such as crabs. Sponges are a favourite of hawksbills.

● **Most turtle species** are under threat because they are hunted for their eggs, meat and shells. The trade in turtles has been declared illegal in most countries, but people continue to kill them.

★ STAR FACT ★
It is believed that sea turtles have been on our planet for over 100 million years. They have survived, while other prehistoric animals, such as dinosaurs, have become extinct.

Loggerhead turtle

Hawksbill turtle

Leatherback turtle

Green turtle

▲ Turtles only come ashore to lay their eggs. Although they are born on land, turtles head for the sea the minute they hatch.

# Sea snakes

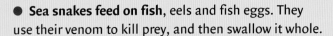

- **Sea snakes** are commonly found in the warm waters of the Indian and Pacific oceans. They can be ten times more venomous than most land snakes.

- **Sea snakes feed on fish**, eels and fish eggs. They use their venom to kill prey, and then swallow it whole.

- **The scales on a sea snake** are small. This reduces friction, helping the animal to swim faster. The sea snake also has a flat, paddle-like tail that aids in swimming.

- **Sea snakes** have to come up to the surface of the water to breathe. They can stay underwater for long periods because they can absorb some oxygen from the water.

- **The sea snake has a gland** under its tongue that gets rid of excess salt from sea water. It also has highly developed nostril valves that can be closed while diving.

- **Aquatic sea snakes** never leave the water, while amphibious sea snakes (sea kraits) slither lay their eggs on land.

◀ *Sea snakes use venom (poison) to stun prey. The venom of sea snakes is more powerful than that of any land snake.*

- **Aquatic (true) sea snakes** are viviparous – the female gives birth to live young.

- **The yellow-bellied sea snake**, named after its bright yellow underside, is the most recognizeable 'true' sea snake. It is poisonous, but attacks only when disturbed.

- **The fastest swimmer amongst sea snakes**, the yellow-bellied sea snake can reach a speed of 3.6 km/h. It can stay underwater for three hours before coming up to the surface to breathe.

- **Sea kraits** have coloured bands on their body. Unlike 'true' sea snakes, sea kraits have wide scales on their bellies that help them to move on land.

# The first boats

- **There is evidence** that boats date back as far as 6000 BC, and maybe even before that.

- **Early boats** were built of wood. In some ancient civilizations, boats were made of animal skin stretched over bones.

- **Coracles** (round boats covered with animal skin) developed later. These had wicker frames and were used for fishing.

- **Kayaks** (another type of skin boat) were used by the Inuit in Greenland for whaling. Kayaks are still used today, but mostly for recreation.

- **Dugouts** made from hollowed-out tree trunks later replaced skin boats.

◀ *The word 'junk' is thought to derive from the Chinese word jung, meaning 'floating house'.*

- **Egyptian rafts** were made from planks of wood tied together. They were used only for trips along rivers and coasts.

- **Sails were first developed** by the Egyptians, in 3500 BC. They equipped their reed boats with square sails.

- **The Phoenicians developed** the sail further. They were traders and needed to travel long distances. During the period 1500–1000 BC, they developed excellent sail boats.

- **Shipbuilding received a boost** during the age of exploration, from AD1000 to 1500. The Vikings and the Portuguese and Spanish sailors went on long voyages, which required fast, sturdy and dependable ships.

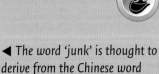

★ STAR FACT ★
Chinese junks had a number of large sails, and were steeredby rudders on the stern. The junks were largely used to transport cargo.

# Ancient cargo ships

- **Three types of early boats** were invented in ancient Mesopotamia (in modern-day Iraq): wooden sail-boats tub-shaped boats called Guffa made from reeds and animal skins, and rafts called kalakku made of timber and inflated animal skins.

- **The kalakku** used currents to float downstream. When it reached its destination, cargo was offloaded and the boat was dismantled and was transported upstream on donkeys.

- **Clay pots** were used as floats. Animal skins were stretched across the inner and outer surfaces of the pots to keep them waterproof.

▶ Ancient Phoenician trading ships had broad beams, a sail and two stern oars.

- **The earliest wooden boats** were simple structures. They were either pieces of log tied together or hollowed-out tree trunks. They could only carry a small amount of cargo.

- **With the need to transport more cargo**, wooden boats were modified. Sails developed in Egypt in about 3500 BC and were used in reed boats built to transport large stones.

- **The invention of the sail** revolutionized shipbuilding, making it possible to move large boat hulls.

- **The Phoenicians were the most skilled** ancient shipbuilders. They made huge merchant vessels, with wooden hulls.

- **Most ancient boats were small**, but ocean-going vessels were made in Asia.

- **Indus Valley people** are thought to have used ships to trade with other civilizations such as Mesopotamia, and Chinese cargo ships (junks) are known to have travelled as far as Africa.

# The ancient Greek navy

★ STAR FACT ★
In the 7th century AD, the Byzantines developed a flaming substance that could be catapulted at enemy ships to set them afire.

- **As the existing merchant vessels** were inadequate for battles at sea, they started to build warships.

- **The Phoenicians** were the first civilization to develop a war galley. They were sailing ships with oars that could be manoeuvred even in the absence of wind.

- **The Greeks** equipped their galleys with bronze-tipped spikes, which could ram into enemy ships.

- **The first war galley** to use the spike was the penteconter, a fast vessel with 50 oars. A penteconter was about 35 m long.

- **About 700 BC**, the penteconter gave way to the bireme. This war galley had two levels of oarsmen, which gave the ship more power.

- **The oars on the lower level** of the bireme were cut into the side of the vessel, and the second level of oarsmen rowed from the deck.

- **The success of the bireme** led to the creation of the trireme – the most effective warship of the time.

- **The bireme** had three levels of oarsmen, with as many as 170 oarsmen in one ship.

- **The Greeks used triremes** to great effect in the Graeco-Persian wars, and were key in establishing Greece as a naval power.

▶ All triremes were named after female mythological characters.

# The ancient Roman navy

● **The earliest Roman navy** was not powerful, and was under the control of the army.

● **In 311 BC**, the Roman navy consisted of a few triremes, but even this was decommissioned a few years later.

● **The Romans developed** a powerful navy about 261 BC, during the First Punic War against Carthage. By this time the triremes were no longer the dominant warships.

● **The Roman navy** had no ship-building experience, so they based the design of their vessels on quadriremes and quinqueremes captured from Carthage.

● **Quadriremes and quinqueremes** probably had one or two rows of oars, with four or five men rowing each oar.

● **These ships often carried** about 100 soldiers and stone-throwing catapults to attack port towns.

● **The Romans also developed** a device called the corvus – a raised board with a spike on the underside.

● **The corvus** was used to board enemy ships. Once on board, the Roman infantry easily defeated the enemy.

● **The weight of the corvus** made Roman ships unstable, prevented the smooth manoeuvring of ships.

● **Some of the Roman navy's strategies** are followed even today. The Romans also pioneered the building harbours at strategic points.

◄ The ancient Romans are known to have recreated some naval battles, at great expense.

# Viking voyagers

● **Vikings** came from the Scandinavian countries of Denmark, Sweden and Norway.

● **The word 'Viking'** means 'pirate raid' in the Norse language. Some Vikings were pirates, but most were farmers who sailed in search of better agricultural lands.

● **The Vikings were the best ship-builders** of their time. They built two kinds of ships: the longship and the knórr.

● **The longship** was a narrow vessel used as a warship. It was about 30 m long, and powered by a single, square sail.

● **Sails** were made of wool or linen, which often cost more than the rest of the ship.

● **Viking women** made the sails. They first made small, diamond-shaped pieces, trimming them with leather strips. These pieces were then sewn together.

● **The knórr was a heavy cargo ship**, about 17 m long. It was used to carry cargo, such as wool, grain and timber.

◄ Viking ships are thought to be the first vessels to have crossed the Atlantic Ocean.

● **When building a ship**, the Vikings first erected the keel – a large beam around which the hull of the ship was built. The keel ran the entire length of the ship, and was made from a single piece of wood.

● **Wooden planks** were fixed to the sides of the keel in an overlapping pattern and then fastened with iron nails, making the ships sturdy and flexible. The floor was set on the keel, and bars were put across to make a deck and seats. The ships were steered by oars at the stern.

● **The bow of the longship** sometimes had a carving of a dragon head on it, so these ships were often called 'dragon ships' by the Vikings' enemies.

# Christopher Columbus

- **Christopher Columbus** (1451–1506) was an Italian explorer who sailed across the Atlantic Ocean to establish a westward sea route to Asia. Instead, this great mariner landed in the Americas.

- **Columbus was only 14 years old** when he first set out to sea. He worked on various ships and even led voyages to Tunisia and Anjou in Africa.

- **After settling in Portugal for a few years**, Columbus moved to Spain with his son. Columbus was driven by a passion for exploring new lands. He made repeated pleas to the Spanish monarchs to fund his expeditions.

- **Initially, Columbus received no support.** The Christian rulers of Spain were more concerned with battling the Moorish kingdom of Granada, than with funding overseas exploration. It was only when victory against Granada became certain, they became more receptive.

- **Columbus once again** approached King Ferdinand and Queen Isabella of Spain. This time he convinced them that he would find a trade route to the Far East.

- **On August 3, 1492**, the Italian mariner finally set sail from Palos, Spain with three ships, Niña, Pinta and Santa Maria. The ships carried over 100 men, ship repairing equipment and other supplies.

- **After sailing for five long months**, Columbus and his crew sighted land. They set foot on an island that they thought was in Asia. But it was actually a part of the Bahamas. Columbus named this island San Salvador.

- **Columbus continued his journey to Cuba**, Haiti and the Dominican Republic. He named the natives 'Indians', since he thought that he was, in fact, in the Indies.

- **On March 15, 1493**, Columbus returned to Spain, where he was accorded a hero's welcome. He was given the title of Admiral of the Ocean Seas and made the governor of all the lands he had discovered.

- **Convinced that Asia** was located beyond the islands he had discovered, Columbus made three more trips to the west between 1493 and 1502. During this period he discovered Jamaica, Trinidad and Tobago, Grenada, Venezuela and Central America.

▼ Santa Maria *was wrecked when it ran into rocks off the coast of present-day Haiti. Its remains were used to build a fort on the island.*

# Vasco da Gama

- **Vasco da Gama** (c. 1460–1524) was a Portuguese explorer who discovered a sea route to India.

- **In 1488**, Bartolomeu Dias discovered the southern tip of Africa, and established that it was possible to reach India by water.

- **To outflank Arab traders** (the primary traders with Eastern countries at that time), King João II of Portugal commissioned Estevão da Gama, Vasco's father, to complete Dias' journey.

- **Estevão died** before completing the voyage. A shortage of funds then put an end to further Portuguese expeditions for a brief period.

- **King Manuel I** came to the Portugese throne in 1495, he decided to renew João's efforts to reach the East and put Vasco da Gama in charge of the expedition.

- **Vasco da Gama planned his journey** and stocked four ships with supplies. He was accompanied by his brother Paolo da Gama, Goncalo Alvares and Nicolao Coelho.

◀ *In 1524, Vasco da Gama was made the Portuguese viceroy to India and set off on his third voyage. He died soon after arriving in the city of Cochin, India.*

- **On July 8, 1497**, da Gama set sail from Lisbon with a crew of 170 men.

- **By December**, Vasco da Gama's fleet had reached the southernmost part of Africa. From there, the fleet continued to sail along the east coast of Africa.

- **Vasco da Gama stopped at coastal towns** to replenish his stocks. Throughout his journey he faced opposition from Arab traders but, with the help of an Arab guide, he crossed the Arabian Sea.

- **On May 20, 1498**, Vasco da Gama finally reached the Indian port of Calicut, which was then the main trading centre for spices and precious stones.

# Ferdinand Magellan

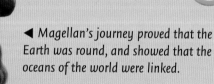

- **Ferdinand Magellan** was born in 1480. He led the first sea voyage around the globe and was also the first European to cross the Pacific Ocean.

- **Like Columbus**, Magellan believed that a westward sea passage to Asia existed. He also realized that he would need to cross the the Americas to find it.

- **Out of favour** with of the Portuguese monarch, Magellan approached King Charles I and told him of his plans to approach the Spice Islands in Asia from the west. Charles I agreed to fund the expedition.

- **On September 20, 1519**, Magellan set sail with a fleet of five ships along the coast of Africa towards Brazil.

- **On December 6**, Magellan sighted Brazil. and continued down the coast of South America towards the Pacific Ocean.

- **In October, 1520**, they found a strait, later to be known as 'Magellan's Strait'.

◀ *Magellan's journey proved that the Earth was round, and showed that the oceans of the world were linked.*

- **It took the fleet** nearly 40 days to cross the straight.

- **It took the fleet** four months to cross the Pacific Ocean. Finally, they arrived at the island of Guam in the South Pacific, where they stocked up on supplies.

- **On March 28, 1521**, they reached the Philippines, where Magellan was killed in a tribal war. His crew carried on with the voyage under the leadership of Sebastian del Cano.

- **On May 1, 1521**, they arrived at Moluccas, or the Spice Islands. They bought spices, and then began the return voyage. On September 6, 1522, one ship carrying 18 crew members arrived in Spain. It was the first to circumnavigate the globe.

# Sir Francis Drake

- **Sir Francis Drake** (c. 1540–1596) was the first Englishman to circumnavigate the globe. He made his living as a privateer (a pirate).

- **Drake commanded his first ship** in 1567 and travelled to the Caribbean on a slave-trading mission. On the way his fleet was attacked by pirates and only three ships survived.

- **In 1572**, Drake led an expedition to make up for the goods stolen by the Spaniards. On reaching the Isthmus of Panama, he became the first Englishman to see the Pacific Ocean. He returned to England a rich and exalted man.

- **In 1577**, Drake was sent by Queen Elizabeth I to capture the Spanish colonies on the western coast of the Americas.

- **Around this time**, Drake changed the name of his ship to *The Golden Hind*.

◄ *Queen Elizabeth I visited Drake aboard the Golden Hind and knighted him for his efforts.*

- **In the Pacific**, the fleet met with dangerous storms, which destroyed one ship and made another unfit for the rest of the journey.

- **When the fleet entered the Pacific Ocean** after crossing the dangerous strait between the South American landmass and Tierra del Fuego, a violent storm destroyed another ship.

- **Drake continued** to sail north. It is thought that he must have crossed California and reached the United States–Canada border.

- **Drake turned west** towards the Pacific Ocean, visiting Moluccas, Celebes, Java and the Cape of Good Hope.

- **When Drake returned home to England** in September 1580, he had become the first Englishman to have sailed around the world.

# The Spanish Armada

- **The Spanish Armada** was a great fleet launched in AD 1588 by Philip II of Spain to invade England and overthrow the queen, Elizabeth I.

- **The Armada comprised** about 130 ships, largely Spanish. Some ships were from Portugal and Naples.

- **The preparation of the Armada** had began in 1586, under the command of marqués de Santa Cruz, but English troops attacked Cádiz in 1587 and destroyed over 30 ships docked at the harbour.

- **The fleet** sailed for England on May 28, 1588. It was the largest fleet ever to be launched at the time.

- **In July 1588**, an English fleet commanded by Lord Charles Howard engaged the Armada near Plymouth.

- **The battle lasted** a week, but the English were unable to break through the Armada's formation.

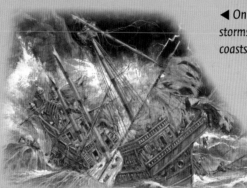

◄ *On its return voyage, the Armada ran into storms. Many ships were wrecked off the coasts of Scotland and Ireland.*

- **When the Armada anchored near Calais**, France, Lord Charles Howard ordered some ships to be set on fire and sent them against the huge Spanish fleet, hoping they too would be ignited.

- **The English fire ships** caused panic among the Spanish and the Armada's formation broke. The English took advantage of this and moved in for the final assault.

- **On July 29, 1588**, the English fleet defeated the Armada in the Battle of Gravelines. About 15,000 Spaniards died in the battle.

- **Only 67 badly damaged ships** of the Armada managed to return home.

# Pirate aboard!

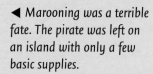

- **The word 'pirate'** means someone who robs ships at sea. Plutarch, the ancient Greek historian, was the first to define pirates in about AD 100.

- **The practice of piracy** is thousands of years old. One of the first surviving documents on piracy dates from 1350 BC. It describes attacks on ships in North Africa.

- **People turned to piracy** for many reasons. Some sailors became pirates after their own ships were captured by pirates, while many simply chose it as a career because it was highly lucrative.

- **Pirates followed the increase in trade** across the world, and many of them established their own empires.

- **Privateering**, which was legal in several countries, also helped the rise of piracy. It was made popular in the 1500s by Sir Francis Drake, the famous British sailor and explorer.

- **Privateers were given a license** to attack pirate ships.

◀ *Marooning was a terrible fate. The pirate was left on an island with only a few basic supplies.*

- **The late 1600s** and early 1700s were the peak of piracy. Pirates flourished in the Mediterranean, Europe, Africa, Asia and the Americas.

- **The Island of Nassau** in the Bahamas played an important role during this period, serving as a resting point for pirates returning from their raids.

- **Punishments for piracy** became more severe in the early 1700s, so it began to decline.

- **It is believed that ancient Chinese pirates** were extremely organized. They kept records of their activities, and even accounts of payments made by their victims.

# Voyages to Australia

- **Maps made after 1540** indicate that European sailors were aware that Australia and New Zealand existed.

- **It is thought** that by this time, Chinese traders may have already made contact with the native inhabitants of Australia.

- **Some Arab countries** may also have traded with the natives (Aborigines) in north Australia.

- **Dutch explorer Willem Jansz** sailed along its coast in 1606, but thought it was an extension of New Guinea, and called it 'Nieu Zelandt'.

- **Another Dutch explorer**, Abel Janszoon Tasman, later use these words to name New Zealand.

▶ *Cook took wildlife experts with him to Australia. They recorded their findings, and collected many plants then unkown in Europe.*

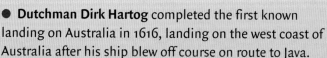

- **Dutchman Dirk Hartog** completed the first known landing on Australia in 1616, landing on the west coast of Australia after his ship blew off course on route to Java.

- **In 1642**, Abel Tasman explored the southern coast of Australia and sighted the island of Tasmania.

- **In 1768**, Captain James Cook sailed around the north coast and east coasts of the continent in his ship the *Endeavour*.

- **Cook made a map of the east coast** and named Botany Bay on the southeast of the island continent.

- **In 1786**, the British decided to colonize Australia, and sent Captain Arthur Phillip there with more than a thousand people, mostly convicts. On January 26, 1788, Captain Phillip established a settlement in Port Jackson (now Sydney).

# Napoleon versus Nelson

- **The Battle of Trafalgar** was fought between a British fleet and the combined fleets of France and Spain.

- **The British fleet** was commanded by Viscount Horatio Nelson. He was appointed commander of the British Mediterranean fleet in 1803 when war broke out between England and France.

- **Nelson's task was to block French ports** to prevent merchant trade.

- **Napoleon Bonaparte**, emperor of France, was nurturing ambitions of conquering Britain, but the blockade prevented this.

- **Bonaparte ordered** the French navy, under the command of Charles de Villeneuve, to break the blockade.

> ★ STAR FACT ★
> It is thought that Nelson suffered from seasickness, and planned his battles far in advance so that he had time to adjust to the sea before he had to fight.

- **Villeneuve reached Cape Trafalgar** near Cadiz in Spain, and formed his ships into a single battle line to break open the blockade.

- **In response**, Nelson divided his fleet into two, and caught Villeneuve off-guard by charging at right angles to the line of French and Spanish ships.

- **Villeneuve was unprepared** for this tactic, so the British fleet was able to easily demolish the French fleet.

- **The battle was over** in a few hours, beginning before noon and ending in the late afternoon.

- **Nearly 20 French and Spanish ships** were destroyed, and Villeneuve was taken prisoner along with thousands of others.

▲ Horatio Nelson was one of Britain's greatest naval admirals.

# Titanic

- **The pride** of the British supping company White Star Line, *Titanic* was built in Belfast, Northern Ireland. It was one of the largest passenger steamships of the time.

- **Around 260 m in length** and 28 m wide, *Titanic* transported passengers between Europe and the US.

- **The ship** had about 900 crew members and could carry over 3000 passengers.

- **In its time**, *Titanic* was the height of luxury, featuring a swimming pool, squash court, library and a Turkish Bath.

◀ *Titanic* took only three minutes to break apart and start sinking.

> ★ STAR FACT ★
> James Cameron's 1997 movie *Titanic* starred Leonardo DiCaprio and Kate Winslet, and was nominated for 14 Academy Awards®, winning 11.

- **At noon on April 10, 1912**, *Titanic* set sail from Southampton, England, towards New York, United States.

- **Four days later**, around midnight on April 14, the ship struck an iceberg off the coast of Newfoundland.

- **The iceberg** ripped through the hull, causing the first watertight compartments to flood. The ship then broke in two, the bow sinking almost immediately. It was followed by the stern.

- **Another steamship**, *Californian*, was anchored nearby. The crew saw the rockets fired by *Titanic*, but failed to recognize them as distress signals.

- **By the time** the liner *Carpathia* came to the rescue, nearly 1500 passengers had died. Only 712 survived.

# Finding the way

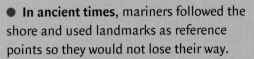

- **In ancient times,** mariners followed the shore and used landmarks as reference points so they would not lose their way.

- **When they began** to venture into the open seas, early seafarers depended on the positions of the Sun and stars to determine their direction.

- **Several instruments,** including the sextant, were designed to calculate a ship's position using the stars.

- **Modified versions** of some of the first navigational tools, such as the magnetic compass, are still in use.

- **The compass** has been in use since the 12th century. It consists of a moving needle that automatically points towards the Earth's magnetic north.

- **The mariner's compass** consisted of an iron needle and a lodestone. The needle was rubbed against the lodestone, then floated in a bowl of water. The needle would come to a rest pointing towards north.

◀ With a sextant, a sailor could calculate his position by measuring the angle and distance between two heavenly bodies.

- **Other early tools of navigation** include the jackstaff, used to measure the Pole Star's distance from the horizon.

- **Ancient navigators** also used a line with a piece of lead at one end to measure the depth of the water, to determine how far out to sea they had sailed.

- **Nautical charts** provided details about bodies of water, such as depth and the location of islands, shores, rocks and lighthouses.

> ★ **STAR FACT** ★
> Early sailors fed reels of rope, knotted at regular intervals, overboard, counting the number of knots pulled off the reel in a given period of time. They could then work out the speed of the ship in knots.

# Diving through time

- **It is believed** that around the fifth century BC, a Greek called Scyllias saved the Greeks from Persian attack by diving beneath the sea and cutting off the anchors of the Persian ships.

- **The origins of the diving bell** can be traced back to ancient times, when divers placed upturned buckets and cauldrons over their heads before going underwater. Inverted objects trapped air inside them, allowing the diver to breathe.

- **Gradually divers began to use** a bell-shaped wooden barrel, which was placed over the diver's head.

- **Air was passed into the bell** through tubes that went all the way up to the surface.

- **The Greek philosopher Aristotle** records that a diving bell was used during Alexander the Great's reign.

- **A more advanced version** of the diving bell is still used today. Modern bells are made of steel and can withstand great pressure.

▶ Early divers breathed through tubes that stretched from their helmets to the water's surface.

- **Ancient Roman divers** recovered treasures from sunken ships, using heavy stones to help them dive to depths of about 30 m.

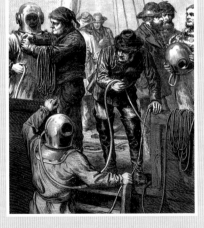

- **It is said that around the first century** BC Roman divers salvaged a cargo of amphorae (ancient wine jars) from the ancient Roman merchant ship, *Madrague de Giens*.

- **Divers were a major force** in naval battles. It is thought that Alexander the Great had to contend with kalimboi (diving warriors) during the siege of Tyre in 332BC.

# Diving equipment

- **The earliest example** of a diving suit is believed to have been made around the fifteenth century. The diver was restricted in how far down he could dive by his air tube, which went up to the surface of the water.

- **It was only in the 18th century** that suits giving freedom of movement were first made. Klingert's diving suit, made around 1797, was one such suit. It was the first to be called a diving suit and comprised a coat and trousers made of waterproof leather.

- **In 1819**, German inventor August Siebe made a heavy-footed diving suit using canvas and leather. The unique feature of this invention was a copper helmet that was supplied with air by a surface pump.

- **Modern diving suits** can be broadly divided into soft and hard types. Soft diving suits are primarily used for scuba diving. They protect the diver from low temperatures but not high pressure.

- **Hard diving suits** are more appropriate for deep-sea diving. They are armour-like suits that have pressure joints to protect the diver from the high pressure underwater.

- **Soft diving suits** are of two kinds – wet and dry. Wet suits keep the body warm. They trap small amounts of water, which is then warmed by body heat. The warm layer of water keeps the diver warm.

- **Divers entering colder waters**, such as the polar seas, wear dry suits. These are made of a waterproof material that keeps the diver dry. Divers wear special underclothes or use built-in electrical heating to keep warm.

- **Some suits have a weight belt** to help divers stay at the bottom. Head gear is equipped with visors and is made of the same material as the suit.

- **The rebreather** revolutionized diving. Invented by Henry Fleuss, an English marine officer, in 1879, this portable air supply system in the form of tanks freed divers from the constant dependence on air supplied from the surface. This was the first self-contained underwater breathing apparatus, abbreviated to scuba.

- **The invention of the aqualung** by Jacques Cousteau and Emile Gagnan in 1942 further popularized diving. A high-pressure cylinder, worn on the diver's back, is connected to the mouth with a hose that has a valve.

▼ Divers control their breathing to make their oxygen supply last as long as possible.

# Modern ships

- **Ships today** are sophisticated fuel-driven vessels. Iron, steel and fibreglass hulls have replaced wooden hulls to provide greater speed and durability.

- **Modern commercial ships** are of various types, but are broadly classified into cargo and passenger ships. Cargo ships are used to transport goods, and passenger liners carry people.

- **Tankers are the most widely used** cargo ships. They are used to transport crude oil, petroleum or chemicals, and are the largest ocean-going vessels.

- **Reefers** (refrigerated container ships) are used for transporting perishable goods, such as fruit and vegetables.

- **Types of boats** include high-speed jet boats, motorboats, iceboats, rowboats and sailboats.

◄ *Frigates are an important part of modern navies. They are used to protect trading ships as well as other warships. They are also a major constituent of anti-submarine warfare.*

- **Oars and sails** are still popular, but motorboats are now more common. They have an internal-combustion engine to provide speed and power.

- **Modern navies** use warships including cruisers, destroyers, aircraft carriers and frigates.

- **Our knowledge of marine life** and resources depends heavily on research vessels. Fitted with state-of-the-art equipment, these ships undertake study expeditions.

- **Specialized ships and boats** are used for fishing, patrolling, repairing and rescue operations.

- **Trawlers, long liners**, seiners and lobster boats have replaced old now fishing boats.

# Modern navigation

- **Today, electronic navigation** is highly accurate and has replaced manual techniques.

- **One of the first forms** of radio navigation was radio direction finding (RDF). Navigators tune into a radio frequency to determine their position.

- **Long-range navigation** (Loran) helps to fix the position of the ship by measuring the time taken by different radio signals to reach the receiver from fixed onshore transmitters.

- **The most popular form of Loran** is Loran-C, which uses two land transmittors simultaneously. This system is now being replaced by the global positioning system (GPS).

- **GPS** is a kind of modern satellite navigation. It uses 24 artificial satellites orbiting the Earth.

- **The navigator** has a GPS receiver. A control device keeps track of the signals received. The receiver calculates the ship's position by comparing data from the satellites.

- **The traditional dead-reckoning system** (DRS) has been modified into the inertial guidance system. This has the same function as the earlier DRS, but is more accurate.

- **Radio detection and ranging** (radar) locates faraway objects by bouncing radio waves off them.

- **A radar uses a scanner** to determine the location of objects. It can also determine its shape, size, speed and direction of movement.

◄ *GPS is used for a variety of purposes such as measuring the movement of polar ice sheets and finding the best route between two points.*

# Modern cargo ships

- **Cargo ships,** also called freighters, are used to transport cargo such as cars, trucks, gas and metals.

- **There are two main kinds** – container ships and bulk carriers.

- **Container ships** carry their cargo in large containers. They carry all kinds of dry cargo, from computers and televisions to furniture and foodstuffs.

- **Bulk carriers** are single deck vessels used to carry unpackaged dry cargo, such as grain and coal. These ships have one large container, and products are poured into it through openings in its roof.

- **Small container ships** called 'coasters' carry small amounts of cargo from minor to major ports.

- **Coasters are named** after the fact that they travel along the coast.

- **Huge cranes** are used at cargo ship docks to speed up the process of loading and offloading cargo. Some cargo ships have onboard cranes (derricks).

- **Roll-on-roll-off** ( RORO) vessels, and lighter aboard ships (LASH) are popular alternatives to container ships. RORO ships have openings on their sides and stern through which cars and trucks can be driven aboard.

- **The LASH vessel** is a cargo ship with its own crane. Cargo is placed in barges that are loaded into a mothership.

- **The vessel can load** or offload several barges near a port. Barges left behind are towed into docks and offloaded at leisure.

◀ *Cargo ships that have fixed routes and charges are known as liners. Tramps are ships that do not operate on any definite route or schedule.*

# Tankers

- **Tankers are huge ships** used for transporting petroleum or natural gas. Some also carry chemicals.

- **All countries** depend on oil and oil products, but few have these natural resources, so oil needs to be transported from oil-rich countries all over the world.

- **Oil pipelines and tankers** are the only two modes of transporting oil around the world. Tankers are one or more tanks designed like a ship.

- **Tankers are divided into various groups** depending upon the nature of their cargo.

- **The largest of all tankers** are the supertankers. They are known as VLCCs or ULCCs. They are about 400 m long and mainly carry crude oil.

- **Supertankers** are the biggest ships in the world. They are too large to approach most ports, so they often have to offload their cargo into smaller vessels.

- **Today some ports** have deepwater offloading facilities that are connected to the mainland by pipelines.

- **Tankers carry millions of litres of oil.** Accidents can cause the oil to spill and result in extensive damage to the environment.

- **Tankers with single hulls** are at the most risk of accidents, since the hull is also the wall of the oil tanks, so a breach in the hull can lead to a major oil spill.

- **Double-hulled tankers** are considered safer because there is space between the hull and the tanks.

◀ *Some tankers have caused huge damage. Oil spills and other accidents can adversely affect the environment and marine life.*

# Container ships

- **This process of using containers** to carry cargo is called 'containerization'.

- **Containerization** was developed in the 1950 by the American Malcolm Mclean.

- **Container shipping** become the method of choice for moving goods from trucks, trains, ships and planes. Today, 90 percent of the world's cargo is moved in containers.

- **The first container ship** was the *Ideal X*, which sailed from New Jersey in 1956.

- **The OOCL SX-class vessels** are the world's largest container ships.

- **The first** OOCL SX-class vessel to be built, the Shenzhen, is 323 m in length and over 40 m wide.

- **Some, called refrigerated ships** (reefers) carry refrigerated containers to transport perishable goods.

- **Reefers** contain insulated compartments and have locker spaces to carry different products at different temperatures.

▲ Cargo is loaded onto container ships by huge cranes that can lift 20–30 containers per hour.

- **If necessary**, some reefers can even provide a humid environment for protecting sensitive products from dehydration.

- **Some reefers** are used to transport medicines, while others are used to keep goods from freezing in harsh climates.

# Fishing vessels

- **People have used boats** for fishing since the beginning of civilization. Commercial fishing may be carried out by a single fisherman, or by huge fishing fleets.

- **Traditional boats and methods** have largely given way to bigger, more advanced vessels and new techniques that produce a very large haul.

- **The three main fishing vessels** are trawlers, seiners and long liners. These are all more than 40 m long.

- **Trawlers**, also known as 'draggers', drag heavy nets (trawls) across the seabed or through the water.

- **Modern trawlers** are powered by diesel. They can measure up to 120 m in length.

▶ Trawlers have refrigeration facilities, so they can keep the catch fresh.

> ★ STAR FACT ★
> The term 'bycatch' refers to animals that are trapped inadvertently in fishing nets. The bycatch is usually not returned to the water.

- **Unlike trawlers**, the mouths of seiner nets are closed before hauling them aboard. Seiners target fast-swimming fish such as tuna and herring.

- **Long-liners** use long lines with baited hooks along their length. These trail behind the ship, hooking tuna, cod and small sharks.

- **Less common fishing vessels** include shrimp or lobsters boats, head boats and dive boats.

- **Modern fishing vessels** are so efficient that their use has greatly reduced the fish populations in many regions. Many countries regulate hauls to slow the decrease in fish populations.

# Luxurious liners

- **Until fairly recently**, ships were the most popular mode of transportation for people. Until the invention of the aeroplane, they were the only way that people could cross the seas.

- **Ships that carry people** are called 'passenger ships'. Smaller vessels are used for shorter journeys, while large ships with lavish amenities (cruise ships) are used for pleasure trips.

- **Cruise ships appeared** towards the latter half of the 20th century. Before that, large, motorized ships known as ocean liners were used intercontinental voyages.

- **Ocean liners thrived** towards the end of 19th century, when millions of people each year emigrated from Europe to the United States. Some of the most famous ocean liners are the *Titanic*, *Mauretania*, *Normandie* and *Lusitania*.

- **The increased use of ocean liners** led to the establishment of shipping companies. The better known of these included the White Star Line and the Cunard line.

▲ The Freedom
*ship is a floating city that
looks like an enormous barge. It
has its own casino, hotel units and even a school.*

- **The Cunard Line** is a British company that owns the famous cruise ships, *Queen Elizabeth 2* and *Queen Mary 2*.

- **The Cunard Line** was the first regular steamship service between Europe and the United States.

- **World War I** severely disrupted the transatlantic service, and some liners were taken over and used to transport troops.

- **After World War I**, France launched the *Normandie* and Cunard launched the *Queen Mary*, but the revival did not last long. The development of jet aeroplanes in the 1950s put an end to the transatlantic ocean liners.

# Ferries

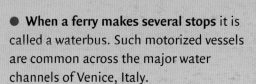

▶ A ferry is a boat or a
ship that transports
passengers over short
distances. Some also carry
vehicles and animals.

- **Ferries** usually have fixed routes, schedules and destinations. They most commonly operate from towns and cities near rivers and seas.

- **They mainly run** across rivers or bays, or from one point in a harbour to another.

- **Long-distance ferries** connect coastal islands with each other, or with the mainland.

- **The Staten Island Ferry** in the New York City harbour is a famous harbour ferry. The most well-known long-distance ferry operates in the English Channel, between Great Britain and the rest of Europe.

- **When a ferry makes several stops** it is called a waterbus. Such motorized vessels are common across the major water channels of Venice, Italy.

- **Ferry boats** dock at specially designed ferry slips. If the ferry transports vehicles, the slip usually has an adjustable ramp.

- **Many ferry services** in Europe use hydrofoils – boats with wing-like foils mounted on struts below the hull. As the vessel picks up speed, the foils lift the hull out of water.

- **One of the best-known ferry services** in the world is the *The Spirit of Tasmania* service, which carries passengers and vehicles across the Bass Strait between Tasmania and mainland Australia.

- **The world's largest ferry operations** can be found in the Strait of Georgia in British Columbia, Canada and Puget Sound in Washington, United States.

# Tugs and icebreakers

● **Tugs, or tugboats**, are small but extremely powerful motorized ships. They are mainly used to guide ships into the docks. They also tow defective ships, barges and heavy equipment across open seas.

● **Although they are known as tugboats**, these are actually small ships and are quite strong despite their size. Modern tugs have diesel engines and can move at a reasonably good speed of 20 km/h.

● **Tugs are also used to haul** oil rigs to new locations, and they can steer huge tankers in and out of oil ports.

● **Tugboats can be divided** into two main groups: habour tugs and ocean-going tugs. Harbour tugs, or short-haul tugs, are used to move ships in the vicinity of the harbour.

● **Ocean-going**, or long-haul, tugs are used to salvage ships from open seas and guide them back to the dockyards for repair, or to tow floating docks and rigs to different locations.

● **Dredgers** are ships that collect sand and other sediments from the seabed. They are often used to deepen channels in harbours to prevent them from getting blocked. The material that is scooped up is used for commercial purposes.

● **Icebreakers are tough**, specialized vessels that are used to clear ice in rivers and seas in order to create a passage.

● **They are very sturdy** and usually quite heavy. They have an armoured body to withstand shocks experienced during collisions with ice.

● **They ram into ice sheets**, or masses of hard ice, and shatter them. Sometimes they crack open an ice sheet by weighing it down with their sheer bulk.

● **Icebreakers help clear the way** so that ships can follow. They are also used for exploration in the polar regions.

▼ *Tugboats are powerful ships and are used to guide ships, such as this aircraft carrier, to new locations.*

# Submersibles and tenders

- **Specialized vessels** such as submersibles, tugboats, icebreakers and dredgers perform tasks that other ships are unable to perform.

- **The submersible** is an underwater research vessel. It is primarily used to conduct underwater scientific research and for military and industrial purposes.

- **Submersibles aid in studies** of undersea geological activity, marine life and mineral deposits. They also help to check on oil rigs. Submersibles involved in research often accompany a research vessel.

- **Navies use submersibles** tasks, such as submarine rescue and repair, and mine detection.

- **Wreck divers use submersibles** for salvage operations, such as recovering planes or equipment that have sunk to the ocean depths.

- **Pressurized submersibles** are designed to operate in very deep waters, and can withstand very high pressure.

- **The sophisticated** submersibles are remotely operated and are equipped with vcameras and sensors.

- **Tenders are ships or boats** that service other ocean-going vessels. Tenders of smaller boats are called dinghies.

- **A ship's tender** helps to transport people or supplies to and from the shore or another ship.

- **Some modern cruise liners** have lifeboat tenders. In addition to serving as tenders, they also act as lifeboats.

◀ The submersible, Nautile, made more than 90 dives into the ocean depths to recover artefacts from the ill-fated Titanic.

# Battleships

- **Battleships** were big, heavily armoured ships with powerful guns. They dominated navies in the first half of the 20th century.

- **During the age of sail**, ships carried heavy cannons, most of which were placed on the sides of the vessel.

- **Since these cannons** could only fire straight, the ships fell into lines, one behind the other. This popular battle formation was called the line of battle.

- **Battleships were rated according** to the number of guns they carried. First-rate ships had three decks with over 100 guns, and second-rate ships carried about 90 guns. Third-rate ships had about 60 guns.

- **Battleship design underwent major changes** during the 19th century. Wooden sail ships were armoured and refitted with steam engines.

- **Towards the end of the 19th century**, one battleship design was adopted across the world – two turrets, four 12-inch guns and smaller, secondary guns.

◀ Chih Yeun, the mighty Chinese battlecruiser, was one of the heaviest and most dreaded battleships of its time.

- **By the end of the 19th century**, ships resembling modern battleships started to appear, beginning with HMS Devastation and HMS Thunderer.

- **Well-known battleships** deployed in World War II were the Bismarck, the Misssouri and the Prince of Wales.

- **During World War II** battleships became secondary to aircraft carriers, which offered greater effective range of attack than the battleships.

- **Several battleships were decommissioned** after World War II. Those retained were largely used as escorts to aircraft carriers or for the bombardment of shores.

# Aircraft carriers

● **Aircraft carriers** are massive warships that carry military aircraft. These ships have flight decks to support the take off and landing of fighters and bombers.

● **Apart from enabling military planes to take off** and land at sea, aircraft carriers also provide air cover to other warships.

● **Most aircraft carriers** have a flat top deck that serves as a strip for take offs and landings. Although it is quite long, it is small compared to normal runways. Hence, steam-powered catapults are used to launch the planes into the air.

● **These catapults** help the planes accelerate from 0 to 240 km/h in just two seconds to attain take off speed.

● **Landing on the carrier** requires great skill. The planes have tailhooks that snag one of four arresting cables stretched across the deck, stopping the aircraft within 100 m.

● **Aircraft carriers are over 300 m long,** with a huge crew. They are expensive, and therefore owned only by a few countries. The United States owns the most carriers. As of 2004, the US Navy has 12 carriers, the most famous being the Abraham Lincoln.

▲ *Most modern aircraft carriers are powered by nuclear energy. The heavier and bigger ones can support over 85 planes.*

● **There are several types of aircraft carriers,** including seaplane tenders, assault carriers, light carriers, escort carriers, fleet carriers and supercarriers. Some of these, such as seaplane tenders, are no longer in use.

● **Most countries today** use light carriers, which can support helicopters and jump jets, or other vertical take off and landing planes. Such aircraft can take off and land with almost no forward movement, and so do not need catapults.

● **Aircraft carriers are accompanied** by many other ships that either provide protection or carry supplies. Together they are called a 'carrier battle group'.

> **★ STAR FACT ★**
> American pilot Eugene Fly was the first to take off from a stationary ship. He did so from the US cruiser USS Birmingham.On May 12, 1912, British commander Charles Samson becamethe first pilot to take off from a moving warship. He did so from the battleship HMS *Hibernia*.

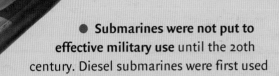

# Submarines

▶ *Modern submarines are mostly cigar-shaped and they rarely surface.*

● **Submarines are warships** that operate underwater. The first submarine was built in 1620 by the Dutch inventor Cornelius Jacobszoon Drebbel, and was propelled using oars.

● **Early submarines** were largely used for underwater exploration. The first submarine built exclusively for military use was named the *Turtle*.

● **Built in the 1770s**, the *Turtle* was a manually-operated, spherical vessel. It was first used during the American War of Independence.

● **Periscopes were added** to submarines in the mid 19th century. Periscopes offer a view of what's happening above water.

● **Submarines were not put to effective military use** until the 20th century. Diesel submarines were first used during World War I.

● **Nuclear-powered submarines** use nuclear energy to stay submerged for longer periods.

● **Submarines also carry weapons** that include mines, torpedoes and nuclear-tipped ballistic missiles.

● **Submerging and surfacing** uses ballast tanks. When a submarine descends, its ballast tanks are filled with water. When it needs to resurface, compressed air is forced into the tanks to push out the water.

● **Attack submarines** usually use torpedoes and are designed to attack warships and other submarines.

● **Ballistic missile submarines** have nuclear warheads to attack land targets such as strategic cities. They are built as back-ups in case all land-based missiles are destroyed.

# Rowing boats

● **Rowing boats** are moved with oars or paddles. The row boats used for sporting activities consist of a long, slender vessel called a shell.

● **Shells used to be made from wood**, but materials such as fibreglass and carbon fibre are more commonly used today.

● **Some rowing boats** are steered by a coxswain, or cox, who sits in the stern, facing the crew. The cox steers the boat and encourages the rowers.

● **Rowing boats** that do not have a cox are called 'coxless', or 'straight'.

● **In kayaking and canoeing**, rowers use paddles instead of oars. Unlike oars, paddles are not used in pairs.

● **Canoes and kayaks** are small vessels with pointed at the ends. Canoes are mostly open-topped, while kayaks are covered.

● **Both canoes and kayaks can be paddled** by one or more people. Kayaks have double-ended paddles, while canoes have paddles with single blades. Despite their differences, people often the word 'canoe' to describe either vessel.

● **There are several sporting competitions** involving canoes and kayaks, including slalom canoeing, rodeo canoeing and canoe polo.

● **Polynesian peoples** once travelled from island to island across the Pacific Ocean in large canoes fitted with outriggers to make them more stable.

◀ *Rowing can be categorized into sweeping and sculling. In sweeping, each rower uses one oar, while in the sculling, each rower uses two oars.*

# Sailing ships

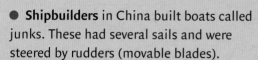

▶ Sailboats are used for cruising, racing or fishing.

● **Sailing ships** use the energy of the wind to move. A sail is made of pieces of cloth stitched together and tied to long poles called 'masts'.

● **The Egyptians** are thought to have developed the first sails. Their reed boats were simple structures with square sails.

● **The Phoenicians**, during the period 1500–1000 BC, developed sailboats further, creating a small space in the hull, called the 'deck'.

● **New sailing vessels** called galleys were developed for use at war. They had rows of oarsmen as well as sails.

● **Galleys gave way** to the bireme, a big vessel that had two decks of oarsmen, followed by the trireme.

● **Shipbuilders** in China built boats called junks. These had several sails and were steered by rudders (movable blades).

● **The Viking** longship was later replaced by 13th-century cargo vessels, called 'cogs', as the major carrier of goods in Europe.

● **In the 15th century**, sturdy four-sailed boats called 'caravels' were developed in Spain and Portugal.

● **Galleons were fast** and had long, slender hulls. The famous *Mayflower*, which took pilgrims to America in 1620, was a galleon.

● **British ships** became larger and more fortified in the 19th century. They were often used to carry riches back from India and Africa.

● **The advent of steam ships** gradually led to the demise of sailing ships. Sailing is now a leisure activity.

# Surfing

▶ Surfing requires great strength and agility and lots of practice. A good surfer has to be extremely fit and be able to swim well.

● **Surfing involves** riding waves using a surfboard.

● **This sport** is usually done in places where big breaking waves are common.

● **Surfers usually lie on their boards** and paddle out to wait for a suitable wave. The idea is to ride a wave as soon as it starts to break.

● **There are several intricate movements** and manoeuvres in surfing. A surfer may ride the crest, or top, of a wave or its breaking curve.

● **The best surfers** can perform manoeuvres in the air. These moves, called aerials, were inspired by skateboarding and snowboarding.

● **In a 360 aerial**, a surfer does a 360 degree airborne spin.

● **Surf boards may be long or short.** The longboards are over 2.5 m in length, while shortboards are 2 m or less. Both have small fins to help with stability and steering.

● **Long considered merely a local recreation**, surfing is now an official sport. Professional surfers generally use the shortboard.

● **Surfing is believed to have originated in Hawaii.** Today, it is a highly popular activity worldwide, especially in Australia, South Africa, the United States and Brazil.

● **In competitions**, surfers are judged by the size of the waves and the distance they ride. Skills shown while performing manoeuvres are also considered.

# Powered for fun

- **With the development** of steam and internal combustion engines in the 1800s, motorboats became fashionable.

- **Some motorboats** use inboard motors, in which the engine is located within the hull. In outboard motorboats, the motor is attached to the stern of the boat.

- **In the water-jet engine system**, water from under the boat is drawn into a pump-jet and then expelled through an opening at the stern.

- **High-speed boats** are used in search, rescue and salvage operations, as well as racing and leisure. Boats like hydroplanes and tunnel boats are especially popular among racing enthusiasts.

- **Hydroplanes** have projections called sponsons at the front. When a hydroplane picks up speed, it is lifted out of the water and supported by these sponsons.

- **The sponsons** of the flat-bottomed tunnel-boat are positioned the sides of the hull. Like the hydroplane, the tunnel boat rises is supported on its sponsons.

- **The runabout is a high-speed motorboat**, which can hold around eight people.

- **Most modern boats** are usually made of plastic reinforced with fibreglass.

- **In jet sprint boat racing**, boats powered by water-jet propulsion race in shallow courses.

- **Offshore powerboat racing** takes place in the open seas.

◄ *Over 14 kinds of high-speed boats are currently used in powerboat racing.*

# Riding the waves

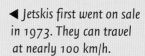

- **In water skiing** the skier is towed behind a motorboat at great speed. Water skiing can be enjoyed on large, relatively calm expanses of water such as rivers, lakes and bays.

- **The sport was invented** by an American teenager named Ralph Samuelson in 1922, who believed that it would be possible to ski on water as on snow.

- **A water ski** run begins with the skier crouched low, holding the tow rope attached to the motorboat. Upon acceleration, the skier stands up straight and starts to skim across the surface of the water.

- **Water skis are made of wood**, plastic or fibreglass. They are generally 1.7 m long and 15 cm wide. Unlike snow skis that have a rigid binding for the feet.

- **There are various categories** in water skiing competitions. In the slalom, the boat runs in a straight line while the skier zigzags around buoys in the water.

◄ *Jetskis first went on sale in 1973. They can travel at nearly 100 km/h.*

- **Trick skiing** is performed using two short skis or a single ski. Participants perform tricks while skiing.

- **In the jump event**, skiers use the ramp to launch themselves into the air while skiing.

- **Show skiing** involves elaborate preparations. With music and colourful costumes, skiers perform dance acts and ballets. Troupes also form complex human pyramids.

- **In wakeboarding**, the rider stands sideways on a board to 'surf' on the waves created by the boat's wake.

- **Jet skis** are motorized personal watercraft that look like motorbikes and travel at high speeds. Most jet skis can accommodate two or three people. The rider sits or stands on the jet ski.

# Oceans in danger

- **Oceans** absorb much of the solar heat and are therefore affected by global warming.

- **Scientists believe** that the enhanced greenhouse effect could cause more water to be formed due to the melting of glaciers and ice caps.

- **Global warming** caused by greenhouse gases has increased the Earth's surface temperature by about 0.6°C over the last century.

- **Higher surface temperatures** can melt mountain glaciers and parts of polar ice caps, causing the sea level to go up by a metre within a century or two.

- **Rising sea levels would affect** coastlines and people and animals living in coastal regions.

- **El Niño**, a sudden surge of warm waters off the west coast of South America, is a significant climatic phenomenon some scientists attribute to global warming.

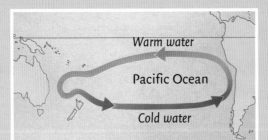

Warm water

Pacific Ocean

Cold water

◀ High atmospheric pressure develops over the Pacific Ocean, causing trade winds to blow from east to west, carrying warm waters towards the west. This is called the El Niño effect.

- **An increase** in the surface temperature of oceans will affect weather patterns.

- **Global warming** is responsible for the melting of sea ice and ice caps in the Polar regions.

- **Oceans are full** of microscopic phytoplanktons, which remove almost half of the natural carbon dioxide formed. Any change in their habitat directly increases the amount of carbon dioxide in the atmosphere.

- **Many nations** are taking action to save the oceans. The Kyoto Protocol requires the countries that have signed it to take measures to reduce the amount of greenhouse gases in the atmosphere by 2012.

# Greenhouse effect

- **Factors affecting marine life** and the environment include pollution, global warming, oil spills and overfishing.

- **The increase** in temperature of the Earth's atmosphere is called global warming. Some scientists think it is the result of the greenhouse effect.

- **The Sun's heat** is absorbed by the Earth's atmosphere and radiated back into space. Gases in the atmosphere trap part of this heat, keeping the Earth warm. This process is termed 'natural greenhouse effect'.

- **Greenhouse gases** include water vapour, carbon dioxide, methane, nitrous oxide, ozone and chlorofluorocarbons (CFCs).

- **Water vapour** is the most important greenhouse gas. It is responsible for over 60 percent of the greenhouse effect.

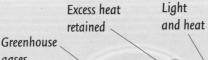

Excess heat retained

Greenhouse gases

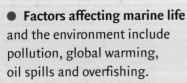

Light and heat

◀ Some of the Sun's heat is trapped by the greenhouse gases in the atmosphere.

- **Greenhouse gases** are crucial, but industrialization has increased their levels, so they trap more heat than required.

- **Human activity** has increased the amount of greenhouse gases. The main factor is carbon dioxide emission.

- **Deforestation** also contributes to the increased levels of carbon dioxide in the atmosphere. Trees that have been cut down release carbon dioxide as they decay.

- **Global warming can cause significant changes** in the climatic conditions across the world.

- **An increase in temperatures** would lead to faster rates of evaporation, the melting of glaciers and polar ice caps, and a rise in sea levels.

# Sinking lands

● **The sea level** has already increased rapidly in the last 100 years due to global warming, with many coastal and low-lying areas threatened by flooding.

● **The major reason** for the rise in the level of the sea is the melting of the Arctic and Antarctic ice packs. The thickness of these packs has reduced in the last century, adding to the volume of water in the oceans.

● **Scientists believe** that the level of the oceans will rise more dramatically over the next 100 years, with temperatures expected to rise by almost 4°C.

● **Many major cities of the world**, such as New York, Los Angeles, Rio de Janeiro, London and Singapore, lie in coastal areas or near river mouths.

● **The constant melting** of mountain glaciers and ice packs could threaten these cities with flooding.

● **Scientists believe** that even a 50 cm rise in the sea level will affect millions of people in Bangladesh, India and Vietnam.

● **The population of small island-states,** such as the Seychelles, the Maldives and Tuvalu, will be seriously affected by a rise in the sea level since these countries are only a few metres above it.

● **Tuvalu** is a group of nine coral atolls that lie in the Pacific Ocean, just 5 metres above sea level. It is predicted that if the present situation continues, then these atolls will be completely submerged within 50 years.

● **Many ecologically sensitive zones,** such as the Everglades in Florida, United States, will become submerged.

● **The rising temperatures** are destroying shallow-water marine life. Global warming is said to be responsible for the destruction of coral reefs in Belize. The Great Barrier Reef off the coast of Australia is also in grave danger.

▼ *The rising sea levels may cause coral reefs, such as the Great Barrier Reef, to become submerged.*

# Bleaching the reefs

● **The impact of global warming** on the oceans is most marked in the bleaching of coral reefs.

● **Reefs are very delicate structures**, formed by coral polyps. The main source of food of polyps is the unicellular algae, called 'zooxanthellae', which live within their tissues.

● **The algae** feed on nitrogen waste produced by corals. They also produce food using sunlight, and it is this that forms the main food of corals.

● **Zooxanthellae** give the reefs their colour, which attracts many other marine creatures.

● **Reefs lose colour and die** when these zooxanthellae are damaged. This is known as 'bleaching'.

▶ *Non-reef building corals (soft corals) are also susceptible to bleaching, but they are able to withstand short-term bleaching much more than hard corals.*

● **Global warming** is the main cause of bleaching. A rise in ocean temperatures interferes with the photosynthetic process, poisoning the zooxanthellae. Corals expel dead zooxanthellae, along with some of their own tissue.

● **Once the algae are expelled,** the corals lose their colour and main source of food.

● **Widespread bleaching** took place at reefs around Okinawa, Easter Island, and in the Caribbean Sea. The Great Barrier Reef has also undergone bleaching in the last 20 years.

● **Some of the coral reefs** that have been permanently damaged are in the warm waters of the Indian Ocean, including those off the coasts of the Maldives, Kenya and Tanzania.

● **Bleached coral reefs** take years to recuperate. Bleaching affects not only the coral reefs, but also a large number of marine creatures that depend on it for food.

# Mineral rich

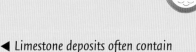

● **The oceans** contain an abundant supply of useful minerals.

● **Sodium chloride** (common salt) is one of the major minerals obtained from oceans. It accounts for 3 percent of the weight of the ocean water.

● **Salt deposits** form when ocean water evaporates. Some lakes and rivers also contain salt deposits and crusts.

● **Other major minerals** obtained from the oceans are magnesium and bromine. Magnesium is compounds are used in agricultural, construction and chemical industries.

● **Bromine is used** in photography, and disinfectants.

● **Sedimentary rocks** such as limestone and sandstone are also found in oceans. They are formed by erosion and are used in building materials.

◀ *Limestone deposits often contain fossils of prehistoric marine creatures.*

● **Huge deposits of manganese nodules** have recently been discovered on the seabed. These nodules primarily consist of manganese and iron. Traces of copper, cobalt and nickel can also be found in them.

● **The oceans** are full of sulphur. Hydrothermal vents spout sulphur-rich water that is also high in other metals and minerals. Sulphur is used in fertilizers, food preservatives, bleaching agents and disinfectants.

● **Mining the oceans** is expensive and difficult. There is an international dispute regarding the ownership of the oceans' mineral wealth.

● **An international maritime law** defines the rules of sharing mineral wealth of the oceans, but the debate continues on whether a particular spot in an ocean belongs to nearby countries or to the global community.

# Fossil fuels

- **Fossil fuels**, such as petroleum and coal, are extracted from the fossilized remains of animals and plants.

- **Crude oil** is formed from microscopic plants and organisms that lived in the ancient oceans.

- **These micro-organisms** died and mixed with silt to form organic mud. Layers of sediment settled on this organic ooze, transforming it into crude oil.

- **Natural gas** is primarily formed by the decaying of dead plankton that have accumulated on the ocean floor.

- **Both crude oil and natural gas** fill porous rocks (known as reservoir rocks) nearby. Since reservoir rocks are normally filled with water, the fuel, which is lighter than water, travels upwards until it reaches a layer of nonporous rocks.

- **The nonporous rocks** trap crude oil and natural gas to create a reservoir of fuel.

- ▶ It takes millions of years for the remains of sea creatures to be transformed into crude oil.

- **Coal is a solid fossil fuel** and is formed from hardened decomposed plants. Coal is often found under the seabed, but offshore coal mining is not as common as that of oil and gas.

- **Scientists have also found** deposits of other hydrocarbon products, such as gas hydrates and oil shale, in the ocean floor.

- **Gas hydrates** are crystals of methane.

- **Oil shale** is a rock containing a waxy compound called kerogen.

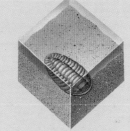

*The trilobite dies and is covered by mud on the ocean floor*

*The fossil forms inside the stone*

# Drilling for oil

- **The search for oil** in the oceans is increasing. Natural resources found in the seabed are extracted and refined to produce fuel.

- **Oil companies** usually build offshore drilling rigs to extract resources from the seabed. Rigs are platforms set up in the sea at a distance from the shore.

- **Oil rigs are** made of steel or concrete that can withstand huge waves and storms. Alaskan oil rigs also have to withstand icy waters and ice floes.

- **Rigs are equipped** with drills that dig several hundred metres into the ocean floor. The samples brought up by these pipes are then tested for signs of crude oil.

- **Once the presence of crude oil is confirmed**, it is extracted and sent to refineries where it is refined into petroleum and petroleum products, such as kerosene.

- **Some oil rigs** are huge platforms, which drop an anchor and float on the water. These platforms have air-filled supports, and are called semi-submersible rigs.

- ▶ The oil platform's legs rest on the seabed. They support the platform above the surface of the water.

- **Permanent oil rigs** are built in places where production is high and multiple oil wells can be drilled.

- **Sometimes pressure builds up** in the underground wells, causing blow-outs. When a blow-out occurs the drilling hole explodes, spilling oil into the water.

- **Oil spills are harmful** to the environment. Apart from polluting the water they also destroy marine life.

- **Blow-out preventers** control pressure in underwater wells while drilling.

# Oil spills

- **Oil spills** are the worst form of ocean pollution. The effects of oil spills are long term and extremely damaging.

- **They are usually caused** when large ocean tankers have accidents while transporting their liquid cargo.

- **During an oil spill**, the oil spreads quickly, forming a thin, film-like layer on the surface, known as an 'oil slick'.

- **Oil also gets into the oceans** from pipelines and underground storage tanks.

- **Oil slicks are harmful** to marine life, as well as to birds and mammals living near the oceans. Oil damages the fur of mammals such as sea otters and the wings of birds.

- **Coral reefs**, mangroves and estuaries are very sensitive to oil spills.

- **The effects of oil spills** can be long-term – for example, they can cause reproductive and growth problems in marine creatures.

- **The oil tanker** Exxon Valdez ran aground in 1989, dumping more than 38 million litres of oil into Prince William Sound, off the coast of Alaska. The damage caused was the worst in history.

- **The environmental damage** caused by the Exxon Valdez prompted the United States Congress to pass safety laws for oil tankers and barges. Oil companies were also made responsible for spill clean-up.

- **In 1978**, by the supertanker Amoco Cadiz, ran aground off the coast of Brittany, France. The spill resulted in one of the largest ever losses of marine life.

◀ *Oil tanker accidents account for barely five percent of the total oil that flows into the oceans.*

# Ocean pollution

- **Excessive human activity** in coastal areas has increased pollution and often caused damage to ocean life.

- **The discharge** of industrial waste and human sewage into the sea is the most common form of pollution. This affects marine creatures and makes the sea unfit for bathing.

- **The pollution** that enters oceans can be categorized as coming from 'point sources' and 'non-point sources'. Sewer pipes and industrial waste pipes are point sources, as the discharge is from a single, identifiable point.

- **Non-point sources of pollution** are harder to tackle. They include water or sewage from farms containing fertilizers with a high chemical content.

- **Some chemicals** found in pesticides are biodegradable, and their effects are minimal. Some remain dangerous for a long time.

◀ *Certain paints used to protect the hulls of ships contain chemicals that are fatal to marine creatures.*

- **Petroleum and oil products** enter the water through spills from ships, and leakages from pipelines and storage tanks.

- **Power plants** are a major source of pollution. The water they discharge is usually hot and so it alters the temperature of the sea water, affecting marine life adversely.

- **The numbers of marine animals** have been diminished by industrial pollution and farm wastes.

- **Many beaches** have become tourist attractions. Plastic litter left on tourist beaches is a great hazard to marine life.

- **Metals such as copper** and lead enter the oceans from industrial waste and automobile emissions, and can cause health problems in animals and people.

# Cleaning the oceans

▶ Sorbents (large sponges) are used in the final stages of a clean-up.

● **The value of the oceans' resources** is now being recognized. Efforts are being made across the world to control the deterioration.

● **The biggest problem facing the oceans** is global warming.

● **Cleaner energy sources** will control the release of carbon dioxide into the atmosphere, reducing global warming.

● **The harm caused by synthetic chemicals** and fertilizers that run off to the oceans, is being reversed by the use of eco-friendly chemicals. These chemicals are bio-degradable – they decompose in a harmless way.

● **Chemical dispersants** break down oil into its chemical constituents, making it less harmful to the marine environment.

● **New devices are being developed** to absorb oil spills – one of the biggest threats to marine life.

● **Oil spills are cleaned** using booms, skimmers and chemical dispersants. On shore, low- or high-pressure water hoses and vacuum trucks are also used.

● **Floating barriers**, 'booms', are placed around oil spills sources to prevent the oil spreading further.

● **Skimmers** are boats with plastic ropes that skim over the surface, absorbing the oil after the booms have been set up.

● **To save coastlines**, many nations are imposing strict building regulations. Construction activity and tourism have damaged many coastal ecosystems.

# Saving ocean life

● **Many marine species** have already become extinct, while many more are endangered.

● **Destruction of habitats**, pollution and overfishing are the main reasons for this.

● **Some ocean regions** are being protected. Fishing and other activities that disturb marine life in these areas are prohibited.

● **These regions have been established** as safe havens for endangered species and the protection of commercial fish stocks.

● **However**, only one percent of the world's oceans are protected. Many organizations, like the World Wildlife Fund, are trying to increase the coverage of protected areas.

● **Some habitats** are protected by the prohibition of destructive fishing gear. This ensures the development of the ecosystem.

● **The Great Barrier Reef** is one of the largest protected marine ecosystems.

● **Drilling for minerals**, oil or gas poses a major threat to sensitive habitats. Efforts are being made to persuade companies to use methods that do not harm sea life.

● **The population of endangered marine species is** being increased by many projects.

● **Turtles, sharks and dolphins**, are being bred artificially under controlled conditions and then released into seas.

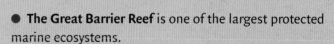

◀ These dead fish are proof of the effects of chemical pollution. Thousands of dead marine creatures are washed ashore every year.

# Endangered species

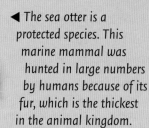

● **Endangered species** are animals and plants that are facing extinction. These species will die out if nothing is done to keep them alive.

● **The main reasons** for a species becoming endangered are the destruction of their habitat, and hunting.

◀ *The sea otter is a protected species. This marine mammal was hunted in large numbers by humans because of its fur, which is the thickest in the animal kingdom.*

● **Around 34,000 plant species** and 5200 animal species are close to extinction.

● **The current rate of extinction** is thought to be around 20,000 species every year.

● **When their habitats are destroyed**, many animals are not able to adapt to the change in their surroundings, which eventually leads to their extinction.

● **Excessive hunting** has greatly reduced the numbers of sea turtles.

● **Between the 1800s and the early 1900s**, whales were killed in large numbers for their meat and blubber. This led to the endangerment of many whale species.

● **Higher water temperatures** have depleted the numbers of several fish species.

● **Changes in biodiversity** can also lead to extinction. Biodiversity is where particular species thrive and depend on each other.

● **The kelp forest in the North Pacific** used to be one of the richest biodiversity zones. When humans killed sea otters in large numbers, the population of sea urchins, the main food of sea otters, increased. The sea urchins then ate more kelp, leading to the collapse of the entire ecosystem.

# Whaling and fishing

● **Whaling** is the commercial hunting of whales for oil, meat and other products.

● **In the 1100s**, whales were hunted off the coasts of Spain and Germany. Whaling in North America began with its colonization and was at an all-time high by the 1700s.

● **In the early 19th century**, whales were usually killed by harpoons and other weapons. Later, large boats equipped with machinery to process slaughtered whales were used.

● **Sperm whales** were killed for the oil they produced, known as spermaceti, used as lubricants and in medicines.

● **The International Whaling Commission** was established in 1946, when whale populations began falling alarmingly. It regulated the hunting of whales.

◀ *The heavy chains that weigh down fishing nets often crush coral reefs and kill other marine creatures in the process.*

● **Fishing** is one of the biggest commercial activities carried out in the oceans.

● **Overfishing** has led to the depletion of many fish species such as cod, mackerel and tuna.

● **The demand** for fish has led to the development of fish farms, where fish are grown and harvested for food.

● **Fish farming** provides about a fifth of all fish eaten – salmon, shrimp and carp are the most harvested.

★ **STAR FACT** ★
Sport fishing is one of the most popular recreational activities in the world. Anglers use fishing rods and lines to catch game fish.

# Crowding the coasts

- **Since ancient times,** humans have made coastal areas their homes. Almost half of the world's population lives close to the coasts.

- **Many coastal regions** are now overcrowded. This has led to pollution, damaged ecosystems and eroded coastlines.

- **People have built houses** and factories that discharge sewage and industrial waste into the seas. These damage shores and pollute oceans.

- **Industrial waste** contaminates bathing beaches and poisons shellfish beds.

- **The development of ports,** roads, coastal construction and mining of sand are destroying coastal habitats like coral reefs.

- **The shore** has also been damaged by attempts to control the movement of sediment such as sand and shingle. This prevents erosion in some places but leads to deposition of sediments in other areas.

- **Jetties and breakwaters** are built to protect harbour entrances and maintain a constant depth of water. These structures block the natural drift of sediment.

- **Artificial beaches** are built to reclaim land from the sea, thus damaging the coast beyond repair.

- **To attract tourists**, hotels and apartments are often built close to the water.

- **This makes such areas vulnerable** to pollution and disturbs the natural marine habitats and marine life.

◄ Littering of beaches is one of the most common problems today.

# Living at sea

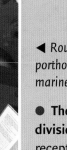

- **Underwater hotels** and artificial islands, such as the Jules' Undersea Lodge and the Palm Islands, have been built to make money from the popularity of islands and seas.

- **The Jules' Undersea Lodge** in Florida, USA, is the world's first underwater hotel. It was named after the French science-fiction writer Jules Verne.

- **Visitors have to dive** over 6 m below the sea to enter the hotel through an entrance in the hotel floor.

- **The Jules' Undersea Lodge** was first designed to be an underwater research laboratory called La Chalupa. Built in a mangrove lagoon, it was used to explore life in the continental shelf off the coast of Puerto Rico.

- **The world's first underwater luxury hotel** is being built off the coast of Dubai. The Hydropolis Hotel will be built on the floor of the Persian Gulf, 20 m below the surface.

◄ Round glass windows that resemble huge portholes provide a wonderful view of the marine life at the Jules' Undersea Lodge.

- **The Hydropolis will have three divisions.** A land station will be the reception. A connecting tunnel will into the depths of the ocean. A submarine complex will be the main hotel.

- **The Hydropolis** will have two transparent domes that will hold an auditorium and a ballroom.

- **The hotel will be built of** concrete, steel and clear Plexiglas that can withstand high underwater pressures.

- **The Palm Islands in Dubai** are two artificial islands in the shape of date palm trees.

- **Each palm island** comprises a trunk, a crown with 17 fronds and a crescent-shaped island forming an arch around them. The palm islands will accommodate luxury hotels, villas and apartments.

# INDEX